C000112415

LET'S TALK ABOUT RACE
(AND OTHER HARD THINGS)

A Framework for Having Conversations
That Build Bridges, Strengthen Relationships,
and Set Clear Boundaries

LET'S TALK ABOUT RACE

(AND OTHER HARD THINGS)

Nancy A. Dome, Ed.D.

LIONCREST
PUBLISHING

LET'S TALK ABOUT RACE (AND OTHER HARD THINGS)
A Framework for Having Conversations That Build Bridges,
Strengthen Relationships, and Set Clear Boundaries

ISBN   978-1-5445-2421-4 *Hardcover*
       978-1-5445-2419-1 *Paperback*
       978-1-5445-2420-7 *Ebook*

To all those who have struggled for decorum and understanding during tough conversations but always knew there was a better way that allowed us to show our true humanity and lead with compassion.

...we are all connected.

...our survival depends on seeing each other differently.

...it's either love or fear.

...let's choose love!

CONTENTS

FOREWORD

BY DR. EDDIE FERGUS

Throughout US Civil Rights history, there has been an ongoing need for a level of competency to have meaningful and impactful dialogue—specifically, dialogue that elicits an opportunity to repair a complicated history of oppression and its ripple effects. Dr. Nancy Dome's Compassionate Dialogue™ through the RIR Protocol is that necessary tool for communities to begin doing this work.

"Rather than trying to label someone as wrong, shame them, or prove your point, the goal (of Compassionate Dialogue™) is to understand one another and then come to a resolution together."

This is what Dr. Nancy Dome writes in this book when

describing how we can approach communicating with one another—especially those with whom we do not see eye-to-eye—and I could not agree with Nancy more. If there's ever been a time in history when we needed this voice of reason, it's now.

In *Let's Talk About Race (and Other Hard Things): A Framework for Having Conversations That Build Bridges, Strengthen Relationships, and Set Clear Boundaries,* Nancy doesn't just write about the urgency of the "why" and the depth of researched theory behind our need for Compassionate Dialogue™. She teaches us the how. That how is the RIR Protocol—something Nancy first introduced me to when, in a training she was doing for a Technical Assistance Facilitators group, she asked us to share our racialized lived experiences. But she did not stop there. She then asked a question that I will never forget: "How do you interrupt that racialized narrative on a daily basis?"

It was the notion of interrupting with compassion—and ultimately, the repairing of what is broken in us and our societies—that set me on my Compassionate Dialogue™ journey and what I believe is needed to bring us back together. As our communities continue to grapple with the intractable nature of oppression and our increasing division, this Protocol is an important tool for individuals to use to develop the capacity to be ready for improving persistently troublesome outcomes involving race, gender, sexuality, language status, and poverty status.

Odds are that you're reading this book for a similar reason to the one that spurred me to work side-by-side with Nancy for the past several years: we want to do our part to repair a complicated history of oppression and its ripple effects, and we see dialogue as the best tool for the job. This starts, at the most basic level, by empowering people like you and me to communicate with others in our day-to-day interactions all the way up to the organizational level to complement diversity, equity, and inclusion activities.

Here—thoughtfully and thoroughly—Dr. Dome shows us the way to do that.

PREFACE

Fifteen years ago, my friend **Dennis O'Donald** and I were sitting on the grass on Mission Bay. Out of nowhere, he turned to me and said, "You know you are supposed to write a book." I simply said, "I know."

And I did know. I have been wanting—no, *needing*—to write a book for more years than I can remember. I literally still have napkins where I outlined the chapter titles that described the ideas that were floating in my head, waiting for me to make time to let them out.

What held me back all those years was that I did not know where to start. And, if I am honest, the whole idea felt very daunting. There were so many things I wanted to write about and so many stories I felt compelled to share that I could not make any logical sense of any of it. Still, I kept hearing the same message that Dennis shared not only that day, but for many years after.

This was not the book in my mind in those days, but it *is* the book that I needed to write now. Every day, it feels like we are becoming more disconnected, and this is my little attempt at being a part of helping us reconnect, of being part of a solution.

The beginnings of *this* book were born when **Dr. Jennifer Jeffries** and I collaborated on a conference presentation that birthed the RIR Protocol. If not for Jennifer, this would have been a short story. I am in gratitude to her for her mentorship when I was junior faculty and for making the time to co-present with me to help me publish and gain tenure, for setting me on this trajectory of creating my Compassionate Dialogue™ Framework, and for always being a supporter, cheerleader, and believer of my work and of me.

Where Jennifer left off, my sister **Dora Dome** picked up. She was my first "Angel" that allowed me to start Epoch Education and ultimately allowed me the time to put the feet underneath the RIR Protocol. As the company grew, so did my understanding of the possible implications of the RIR Protocol: to be an equalizer for those who sometimes feel powerless in their ability to navigate difficult conversations. I am in gratitude for her unwavering love, commitment, and belief in me and what Epoch could be—

even though we do not always practice Compassionate Dialogue™.

Shortly after we founded Epoch, cash flow was tight and without missing a beat, **Mark Kelley, Rudell O'Neal**, and **Julie Fenster** became investors to ensure we could grow without struggling. All they had was a promise that I would pay them back and that was enough for them to take the risk. Without each of you, Epoch might still be a dream, so I want to thank you for sharing the vision and choosing to be a part of its creation.

Then there is the plethora of those who have, in one way or another, shaped me and my work by holding me accountable, providing support, and giving me unconditional love (along with the occasional one raised eyebrow to say, "Hm, I'm not sure about this.") Not in any particular order, this includes: **Tom Flaherty**, who jumped on my bandwagon without really knowing me but who trusted his instincts that my idea was worthy of his support; **Carlos Gomez**, who created animated themes for the first iteration of The Epoch Conversation Staters Cards; **Suzanne de Rosa**, who was there from the beginning of the Conversation Starter Cards™, muddling through the GoFundMe and handling the design and fulfillment of the first decks. She has been my right-hand woman, stepping in whenever and wherever needed. Thanks for sticking with me and for simply being you; **Ezra Dweck**, who (somewhat) patiently taught me how to produce a good quality video that would not turn people off and also who continues to give generously of his time to help bring the RIR Protocol to life; **Deanna Furlong**, who has been the necessary constant critical eye as the RIR Protocol started to take shape on social media; **Tim Freeman**, who helped me conceptualize the business model and allowed me to interview him in one of the first Conversation Starter videos I posted on YouTube; **Leigh Ann Peeleman,** who has cheered me on every step of the way and who proofed the final version of this book, being direct and asking clarifying questions as only a bestie can; and **Claudia Bishop**, who gave me my first lesson in separating the person from the behavior when we were college roommates, and continues to be a true friend and supporter of my endeavors. I love you all, and I would not be the person I am today without each of you in my life.

More recently, the additions of **Susan Callender** and **Kelly Cole** to the Epoch Team has been a game changer. They have helped transform our work anchoring Compassionate Dialogue™ at the center of all that we do, breathing into it new life and possibilities. Specifically, it was Susan who said, "If you really want to do it, I'm going to make it happen!" Six months later, I am writing the dedication to my first book that is not my dissertation. You two are my rocks!

And **Taylor Arnot**—my husband, friend, lover, and greatest supporter of all my endeavors—simply thank you for being you and for loving me.

Finally, I need to thank from the bottom of my heart, my editor **Jessica Burdg** who stood beside me on this journey. She held me accountable to meet my deadlines, gave me valuable insight and input on the myriad things I was clueless about when it came to writing a book, and always showed up with love, kindness, and humor. You are reading this book because of her.

I know I have missed some important mentions, but please know it is not because you do not matter enough. Rather, it is because my brain function is not what it used to be, and I simply cannot filter through all the noise to get to the necessary details to recall what I know is there.

This book is possible because of all of you!

To my readers: I sincerely hope this book inspires each of you to allow for vulnerability, step into discomfort, and build bridges. And who knows, maybe those other books can now follow.

In gratitude,
Nancy Dome

INTRODUCTION

WHY CAN'T WE JUST TALK?

"All conservatives are racists."

"All liberals are socialists."

"We all know Blacks and Mexicans are more likely to be criminals."

"I would never have guessed you were gay!"

"Women shouldn't be leaders. They're too emotional."

"She's so unprofessional. She must be a millennial."

There are two ways to look at how we communicate today:

you could say we've come a long way...which we have. You could also say we have a long way to go...which we do. This is the first of many examples in this book that show more than one thing can be true at once—a concept that is still hard to grasp for so many of us; just one piece of what hinders our collective (in)ability to communicate effectively.

How do I know? Because I've made it my life's work to not only understand what's at the root of this problem, but also to find a way to fix it. And a fix, by the way, is desperately needed. Today, miscommunication runs rampant across the country. Political correctness (PC), which took hold in the nineties, has rendered us all but ineffective in our pursuit of communicating with one another. There is more gossip, hurt feelings, misunderstandings, and intolerance because we do not actually know how to engage with one another when the going gets tough (as evidenced in the statements you read a few seconds ago). We are great when all is well, but if history has shown us anything, it's this: all is definitely not always well. What then?

Why, then, can't we just talk? This is not a simple question with a simple answer. We all bring our personalities, learning styles, and lived experiences to the table. These factors and others—such as to whom we're speaking, power dynamics, and how we feel in the moment—all influence how we communicate, and rightfully so.

There *is* a path forward, though. That path is Compassionate Dialogue™. And because we know the right way forward can feel indistinct sometimes when it comes to these tricky interactions, I've also developed a protocol within Compassionate Dialogue™ that acts as a signpost when you need it. A compass. A gut-check. It's called the RIR—Recognize It, Interrupt It, Repair It—and I'm going to teach it to you in this book.

WHY SHOULD I READ THIS BOOK?

When was the last time you felt frustrated or overwhelmed or faced an uncomfortable situation you didn't know how to handle? Did you walk away from a conversation, perhaps one that included language like the statements at the beginning of this book, quietly disgusted by what you heard? Did you write the person off in your head and leave? Did you blow up in anger? Did you feel guilty inside about not saying anything? Did you feel guilty inside because you *did* say something, but you felt it could have gone better? All of these possible responses—of which there are far more, of course, because humans are complex—are alike in a key way: you're upset and frustrated. Not only that, but you didn't change anything for the better. Lose-lose.

The RIR Protocol shows us there is another way. A better way. A more humane, compassionate way to engage, disagree, heal, grow, and move forward. So often, we get blocked by fear—fear of not saying the right thing, fear of retaliation, fear of not having the right information, fear of not knowing enough, or fear of not having the right to speak on a topic. All these barriers get in the way of effectively engaging with one another. I will teach you how to remove those barriers by proposing a new way to approach these conversations—a way that says you don't have to have all the answers. Instead, you simply have to self-reflect, check in, ask questions, and commit to staying engaged.

When we think we need all the answers, we approach conversations defensively. We spout statistics or a litany of examples. With the RIR Protocol and Compassionate Dialogue™, though, we genuinely seek to understand. Too often, people disagree but have no desire to understand each other—but if you desire to understand, instead of trying to be right, you inquire. That curiosity opens you to learning and growing instead of simply getting triggered and reacting.

There is hope for another way of interacting. The way we talk to each other personally as well as on an organizational and societal level needs to change. It can and should be different. How many times have you watched a toxic argument on social media and wondered why people speak to each other this way? Why don't we have any tolerance for difference? Why are we so hateful? Many well-meaning people know there must be a better way; they just don't know what that way is. If you're still reading, I'm betting that's you.

Note that this book is not a guide on how to "win" an interaction. I don't want to weaponize the RIR Protocol, which can happen in the name of "wokeness." Some people think once they're woke, they get to call others out. I founded my national diversity, equity, and inclusion (DEI) company Epoch in 2014, and in the nearly 500,000 clients we've worked with, I've reminded my share of people that the first part of any of this is compassion. People threatening to "RIR each other" doesn't help make the world a more equitable place. The RIR on its own, without the compassion, is just another argument full of shame, blame, or ulterior motives.

WHAT TO EXPECT

All told, this book offers a tool to improve your communication skills in a big way, benefitting you personally, those you are in relationships with, and society as a whole. If you can take in even a fraction of the material you'll learn here and test it, even on a surface level, I guarantee it will make an impact. I've also included an appendix of resources if you want to take a deeper dive. Either way, once you try the RIR Protocol and it clicks, you don't forget it. You may forget the acronyms, but this book will change how you see and move through the world.

I know because it has for me.

Truthfully, Compassionate Dialogue™ has transformed my life. I was born a fire horse and a Sagittarian—my arrows shoot straight and hard. I have to share this information to set the context that what follows out of my mouth might be a little rough. Today, I'm still direct, but the RIR Protocol has softened my edges. I never communicate out of malice or aim to hurt anyone, even when I'm angry. I've always wanted to be honest and direct, and the Protocol helps me form what I have to say in a way where people can hear me, with less defensiveness and hurt. It's also empowering, allowing me to frame my communication in that way doesn't change my truth.

Sometimes we get stuck in our righteousness to the point of weaponizing our communication. In fact, though, we *can* tell our truth in a way that avoids unnecessary harm.

We *can* communicate in a way that inspires growth. My experience and input don't need to diminish the person I'm talking to, even if I don't agree. I'm offering another way, not *the* way.

Remember what I said at the very beginning of this book? We've come a long way AND we have a long way to go. Both true. Let's get started.

CHAPTER 1

WHERE DOES COMPASSIONATE DIALOGUE™ COME FROM, AND WHY DO WE NEED IT NOW?

My first year of college in Arizona, I'd just turned eighteen. Some friends and I were driving from a bar in Casa Grande back to their apartment in the same town. I was in the back seat and the only Black person in the car; the other three were young White men in their twenties, and I was trying to date one of them. You can remember being eighteen and infatuated, right? Anyway, on the way, the two in the front seat stopped at a Circle K convenience store to get some beer. They knew the cashier and decided they didn't like her attitude that night, so they took the doormat on the way out as a prank and teased her about it.

This evening sounds like a typical college experience, but it took a turn that changed the course of my life.

Even though the clerk knew these young men, she got angry, called the police, and said they'd stolen from the store. They were honestly just playing a joke on her and planned to bring the mat back the next day, since they lived nearby. At that point, though, the situation spun out of their control. The police pulled us over, searched the car, found a roach from a joint in the ashtray, and arrested all four of us.

Mind you, I'd never been in the car with this group before, but now I was getting arrested for their small amount of drugs I'd known nothing about. As the only woman, the police took me to a different facility and strip-searched me. I found out later the three guys got searched, but they didn't have to take off their clothes.

We stayed in jail overnight, where I spent the whole time crying in fear, while my friend tried to calm me by talking to me through the vent in his cell. The next day, we each met individually with the judge. The judge asked the driver for his plea to the charges, and he said he pleaded guilty, but the two of us in the back seat should not face charges because we were just getting a ride home. We didn't even know about the stolen mat until the police pulled us over. The judge said the driver would get a weekend in the state penitentiary, to which he replied, "Then I'm changing my plea. I'm not guilty and not going to the state pen for a prank. I'll get a lawyer." The judge set his bail at $175.

The passenger in the front seat pleaded guilty, not to the drugs but to taking the mat, and reiterated that the two of us in the back should not be charged. He got sentenced to a weekend in the penitentiary. He was nice guy from Texas (but I got the impression it was not his first tangle with law enforcement), so he didn't argue. He said it was just a joke but that he would take his sentence because he did take the rug.

The young man I was interested in explained he'd had no idea what was going on until the police pulled us over, because he was just getting a ride home. He pleaded not guilty to everything, and the judge released him on his own recognizance, with no bail.

I also pleaded not guilty and explained I was only getting a lift home because the friend I'd gone with had left me without a ride. I said I didn't know about the theft and didn't do drugs. The judge set my bail at $275. My saving grace was the guy I was infatuated with being let out on his own recognizance, because when he got out, he drove to my college, found my roommate, who then found a teacher who agreed to post my bail, even though she'd never met me. She simply understood I had to get out of there.

PICKING MY BATTLE

I called my dad, who encouraged me to come home. I couldn't, though, because then I couldn't play volleyball, which paid my tuition and allowed me to attend college. My dad didn't raise me, and we had just met a couple years before, as adults. Even so, he sent me the money to pay for the bail and hired me a lawyer. The lawyer didn't want to settle because he said my case was obviously a false arrest. He actually wanted me to countersue.

But I was eighteen and scared, so I declined to fight and signed a covenant saying I wouldn't later sue the state of Arizona for false arrest. The lawyer strongly advised against it, because he said I'd been treated unfairly and there was obvious bias in the way the judge set my bail so much higher than the others'. My dad told me not to worry, though, and supported me in picking my battles.

My entire life, I've regretted that decision—not because I missed out on a financial reward but because it allowed a system to continue to victimize people like me. Had I been outspoken and put pressure on the system, I could have made a positive impact. I could have refused to let the issue go and exposed the inherent racism in our different treatment.

I think about that fork in the road and my choice all the time. In fact, it influences the decisions I make today. Sometimes I don't want to stand up and don't have the energy, but I know my actions don't just affect me. All of our actions have rippling effects, and people down the road can and will benefit from what I do right now.

UNEQUAL OUTCOMES

I settled, and the friend who pleaded guilty spent two days in the state penitentiary. The other two had to go back to court, so I went to support them. A different judge heard their case, and they again explained the mat had just been a prank. The cashier had been angry and taken out her feelings on them, but the situation had spiraled out of proportion. They said they would never steal from a store they lived right next to and visited all the time.

The judge said he couldn't care less about the mat from the Circle K, but he wanted the officer to identify the quantity of drugs involved—a dime bag, a pound, a kilo? The officer said, "Well, it was a roach." The judge was incredulous. He said, "You arrested four people using taxpayer money and put them in jail overnight for a *roach*?" He threw the case out and reprimanded the police officers.

The two men felt relieved to have the charges dropped, because they were in graduate school for aeronautics and couldn't have a criminal record. I, on the other hand, had already spent money I didn't have and shouldn't have had to simply because I felt like I had no other recourse. I was too young and scared to fight what felt like an uphill battle against unequal treatment.

The female officer who strip-searched me seemed extremely harsh. In the moment when I was separated from my friends, I didn't consider that I was receiving different treatment and basically assumed the same was happening to them. Later, when we compared notes, I saw the disparity. I didn't experience brutality or endure slurs, but the difference in treatment could only be attributed to being a Black girl with White guys in an area that did not condone the mixing of races. I was in shock. I could not believe I was being arrested when I'd never been in any kind of trouble. By being in the wrong place at the wrong time, I found myself thrown in a jail cell with criminals. Later, I saw the racial element as well.

This experience represented an inflection point for me, when I realized I would be an advocate for civil rights. I didn't yet know I would become an educator. My treatment forced me to face how much inequality people endure every day. In hindsight...I got off light.

FINDING MY CALLING IN EUROPE

After finishing my first year in Arizona, I applied to a couple of universities in California and received a full scholarship to pursue my undergraduate degree at United States International University in San Diego, an international school with additional campuses in Kenya, Mexico, England, and Japan. Students could transfer their credits to any of the affiliated campuses, which allowed us to travel the world with all our school expenses being paid. This appealed to me for many reasons: one, I could continue my education because the experience in AZ almost threw a wrench in my ability to get another athletic scholarship; and two, I had (have) a bit of wanderlust. The thought of having access to the world in a way that I never thought would be possible due to our financial situation growing up was exciting.

My mother left when I was eleven and moved to Europe. It was traumatic for all of us, and it left me with a lot of anger toward her. One thing I realized early on, however, was that living with that kind of anger toward my mom was not healthy for me, so I decided to spend half of my sophomore and junior years of college in England to be closer to her and get to know her better. I wanted to understand why she left and figure out a way to mend our relationship. During my senior year, I got offered a job to coach softball and volleyball at the England campus in exchange for paying for my master's when I graduated, so I moved to England full-time in 1988 to pursue a degree in social work.

I've always been very people centered and social. I'm an identical twin, but I was the outgoing one, the daredevil, the risk taker. When I went to Europe for the first time, I had ten dollars in my pocket. My brother asked what the hell I thought I was doing. I said I could be poor in San Diego or poor in England, and I was choosing England. I bought a round-trip ticket, then once I arrived, room and board were covered. At that time, the school would pick students up from the airport, so I didn't even need money for transportation. In hindsight, I'm probably lucky my parents weren't there to stop me. I never want to look back and wish I had done anything differently, so I tend to forge ahead and pay the piper if I need to later.

When I moved to England for my master's, I learned the program had been canceled due to lack of enrollment. They had sent a letter to the school in San Diego, but I'd already graduated and never received it. Since I was already there, the school offered me a choice of pursuing a master's in business administration or curriculum and instruction. Since I had no interest in business and didn't want to leave school (remember, I have wanderlust), I chose a master's in education focusing on curriculum and instruction.

After a year, I felt burned out on school and decided to take a year off. I happened to be on the cover of a volleyball magazine in England when an international coach saw it and asked if I was interested in playing pro. It was truly an answer to my prayers to be able to travel and take a break from school. So, I moved to Belgium to play pro volleyball. I was twenty-one and started getting in a little trouble drinking all the good beer in Belgium. The team was considered a semi-pro team, comprised of two fully compensated athletes while the rest of the team received payments for practices and matches. I was one of the full-time pro athletes. We only practiced two nights a week, which left me with a little too much time on my hands. In 1990, a nearby American military base was looking for a substitute teacher, who had to be American for admittance onto the base, so I filled up some of my spare time and put my master's coursework into action by teaching kids who had been expelled from the classroom. I was essentially a detention teacher, but I loved it.

I believe if you let go of attachment to the "way" something needs to unfold or looks and are open to following where you're guided, you usually end up where you're supposed to be. I didn't fight the degree change, and then even though I'd switched to sports, I found myself back in the teaching field...or should I say, teaching found me. Maybe God or the universe was telling me something. Before those experiences, I'd never thought about being a teacher. In fact, I would have said, "Hell, no," if anyone had asked. As it turned out, though, I loved everything about it, including the kids with the greatest challenges.

The next year, the team in Belgium folded. I went back to England to finish my degree, and then I returned to California in 1992. I went into childcare work because I still thought I'd become a social worker. However, I quickly realized social workers don't have enough resources and the system is broken. I was still very committed to working with youth, especially those most marginalized and at risk for school failure. So, through a series of lucky interactions, I discovered the Juvenile Court and Community Schools. I knew that it was, in fact, the educational side of this work that I was being called to do. That year I worked as a childcare worker, which gave me time to go back to school at night to get my teaching credential.

When I think about why I ended up working with children, my family dynamics definitely had an impact on me, but my desire to help people predated my mom leaving. I had the most amazing foundation growing up in West Hollywood, including consistent friendships from early childhood through graduating from high school. I understood community and appreciated how we took care of each other. My upbringing in a close-knit neighborhood taught me to look out for my community like family. I wanted to bring that sensibility to my work, and more importantly, to the kids I hoped to serve. I would spend the next ten years teaching some of the most amazing students I could ever hope to work with. On some level I think they taught me more than I taught them, but the most important lesson was understanding the value and importance of building relationships first and foremost in the teaching and learning process.

"NON-NESS" LIGHTS THE FIRE

Eventually, I became a professor at California State University–San Marcos, and presenting published papers at conferences was one of the requirements for earning tenure. I was slated to co-present with a colleague at the National Association for Multicultural Education (NAME) conference, and we were brainstorming about the topic.

My co-presenter, Jennifer, described seeing signs at a hiring event upon entering a County Office of Education shortly after she retired from being a district superintendent. One said, "Certificated Applications," with an arrow pointing one way, and the other said something to the effect of "Nonessential Personnel." She was shocked and commented on the language being used to recruit district employees. We really just couldn't believe a district could hire someone full-time for the benefit of the students but label the work "nonessential."

We talked about that language mindset, and I said it's "*non-ness*," like being "non-White" or a "non-English speaker." People of color are constantly defined by what we're *not*, instead of what we are. This approach comes from a deficit mindset that holds that those outside of the narrow White normative norms are somehow deficient. I become non-White instead of being Black. Those two labels differ greatly. Instead of identifying people by their support roles as bus drivers or cafeteria workers, they're "nonessential personnel." So, we created a training called the "Tragedy of Non-ness," which is, of course, a made-up word for a real phenomenon. The training goes a long way in encouraging a person to become more aware, through the play on words, of the language being used.

The dynamic is so insidious we don't even recognize it's happening, but there's a detrimental impact to constantly wearing labels based on what you're not. Jennifer and I created the presentation and wanted to consider how to interrupt such language patterns. We talked through it and realized you have to recognize there's a problem, then you have to interrupt it, and then you have to repair it. The repair piece was important, because it takes significant effort to stay engaged after a confrontation, while recognizing and interrupting come more naturally. The audience responded so well to the presentation that the conference invited us back the next year to do a full-day training, which meant we had to flesh out the content and drill down into exactly what the work would mean.

That conference marked the birth of the Recognize-Repair-Interrupt (RIR) Protocol. It wasn't called Compassionate

Dialogue™ at that time, just the RIR. We never progressed much beyond the training, but after a couple of years, I realized I'd started to live it. I practiced it myself in my everyday life. I approached Jennifer and said I wanted to develop the program further, and she gave me her blessing.

I had to ask myself what the framework would look like and how I conceived of the goal of the RIR. Most broadly, I wanted people to have tools to compassionately communicate with each other. That's why I trademarked Compassionate Dialogue™ and started clarifying how it could look as a tool.

I've been using the RIR Protocol for about fifteen years at the time of this writing, and the past nine represent some of the most in-depth work on its development. Then, when I co-founded Epoch Education, it became one of our pillars. I started the organization because I wanted to make a difference without the constraints of having to try to do so through someone else's vision that may or may not fully align with my own.

RESOLUTION AND SELF-CARE

Compassionate Dialogue™ is ultimately about grace. If someone doesn't want to engage with me anymore and can't get past an issue, it doesn't matter whether they know or use the RIR Protocol. I know it, and I live it. I can find a resolution for myself and move on in a healthy way consistent with my values.

One of the biggest benefits of the RIR Protocol is self-care. It offers a way to take care of ourselves and set boundaries regarding how we engage with people and what we allow in our lives. If someone violates those boundaries, we have this process to help us clear the air and move forward. Part of why people are so disgruntled with each other is because they're waiting for the other person to either apologize or forgive them. If the other person can't or won't deliver that closure, then how can we move forward anyway, through forgiving them or ourselves?

Ideally, both parties would participate in the RIR process, but the beauty of using the RIR Protocol is you don't *need* the other person to be a part of that equation. You can't make someone engage with you, but you can always take responsibility for resolving the situation yourself. If you don't, you'll continue to carry that baggage around. Nearly all of us can think of one or two things from the distant past that still stick with us and we wish we'd handled differently. Those memories linger because they're unresolved.

Staying grounded in the RIR Protocol promotes self-regulation, which leads to self-care. If I can use the RIR Protocol and regulate myself, my choice of words, and how I choose to engage, then others don't control my feelings or my actions and trigger me. Suddenly I have the ability to care for myself and make my own choices. External factors don't steer my life, and I can decide whether and when to engage.

I've messed up more than my share, I assure you. Most of my mistakes don't weigh on my conscience, though, because I've been able to resolve them through the RIR. It doesn't matter how long ago you made a mistake, whether you were an adult or a child, whether two days ago or twenty years ago. If you're still thinking about it, it's unresolved. There is some form of regret, shame, or other unprocessed feeling. How many of us in the world are still carrying things that are actually long gone? Wouldn't it be nice to finally set them down?

STRONGER RELATIONSHIPS

Collectively, by using Compassionate Dialogue™ within our organizations and groups, we begin to build trust, safety, and belonging. The RIR Protocol allows us to honor each other and meet people where they are, without expectations about where we want them to be. We're having an honest dialogue.

When you build that trust, safety, and belonging, you promote sustainability and consistency. I don't have to worry about how we'll communicate with each other when you see me. I don't have to fear abandonment if I do something wrong. Together, we establish a new norm. It's sustainable because people feel valued and appreciate that they're being heard.

As a result, we can truly, authentically engage with each other. More importantly, we can fail and learn from that failure without being condemned. So many people are unwilling to take risks, because they feel like if they make a mistake, they'll be condemned. However, if we use the RIR Protocol and meet people where they are, we start to create a safe climate and culture that encourages both risk-taking and feedback. We become used to giving and receiving input.

Receiving feedback is more difficult than giving it, because we are so unaccustomed to people critiquing us. A short-coming of our PC culture is we don't give people honest feedback anymore. The reason we talk *about* people is because we don't talk *to* them. If I give you the feedback you need, there's no reason for me to go behind your back and say what a horrible job you're doing. That direct communication benefits everyone collectively.

The new culture builds empathy and understanding, while allowing us to set boundaries and expectations. We collectively develop a responsible way of engaging with each other that yields stronger and healthier communication dynamics and ultimately, relationships.

INDIVIDUAL GROWTH

As an individual, I use the RIR Protocol to help stay grounded and centered in difficult conversations. It's my North Star. Instead of reacting, I can respond thoughtfully, because I'm conscious of what's happening in my body. I drive the conversation instead of letting my body take over and follow whatever impulses it wants to. Remember, I am a Sagittarian and a Fire Horse...unchecked impulses are *NEVER* pretty for me!

It's important to understand that using the RIR Protocol doesn't magically make the rage disappear. However, instead of the rage controlling us, we control the rage because we're grounded.

The RIR also helps me manage my expectations of others. Usually when we enter difficult conversations, even though we say we're not trying to change people, we really are. When I use the RIR Protocol, though, I'm sincerely not trying to change you. It reduces my expectations that you'll change to my perspective or be different. My only expectation is that we hear each other, which prevents setting myself and the conversation up for failure. If I think you're supposed to change because you've heard my story and then you don't, I'll be angry for a whole new reason— because you didn't meet my expectation.

The RIR Protocol also provides guidance for why we're

having a conversation in the first place. When we talk about Compassionate Dialogue™, we always ask, "Why are you interrupting?" It's essential to think about the "why." In typical, ungrounded conversations, we interrupt someone or something to make a point. We want to shame or blame the other person or prove them wrong. Coming from a more centered, compassionate place, the reason becomes to truly understand the other person and move forward. The why becomes clear, and it focuses on connection rather than a power struggle. We can feel passionate about an issue without trying to control others.

There are times when the slight, or "thing," is just too much, and honestly, I am too tired to try to understand. In these situations when I experience what I call "race fatigue," I try not to interrupt. If I'm enraged, the interruption would be pointless. If I can't come from a place of seeking to understand, then it is simply better not to engage. Engaging with the wrong motivation would set me (us) up for failure—or, worse, could actually degrade into a dangerous situation. Sometimes choosing not to engage is necessary, because it's better than reacting, cussing someone out, and still not being closer to a resolution. However, the key word here is "choosing," which in and of itself is empowering. So regardless of whether I choose to interrupt or disengage, the RIR Protocol brings a level of consciousness that allows me to control my actions rather than letting my actions control me.

As a result, the RIR Protocol increases our efficacy as individuals. If we follow the steps, our communication is far more effective than if we don't. It creates more space for connection, because if I try to meet you where you are and seek to understand, then we'll more likely hear each other and meet in the middle.

THE PURSUIT

I recently conducted a training with a group of women. A White woman in her seventies described being in the post office in Glen Ellen, California, after President Biden's inauguration, and seeing a younger woman walk in wearing a MAGA hat and MAGA shirt. The woman from my training said, in a joking (rather than threatening) way, "You're brave wearing that in here." She knew the younger woman was a fish out of water in this community. They ended up having an amazing dialogue, and in the end, the young woman thanked her for being the first person to talk to her and try to understand where she was coming from rather than just flipping her off. They didn't change each other's minds about MAGA, but they both left feeling more connected. They saw each other as people instead of simply behaviors they didn't like.

Author and lecturer Dr. Gholdnescar Muhammed shared an idea that deeply resonates with me. Historically, Black literary groups from the 1800s always talked about the pursuit of education. (Why we don't know about these groups today is for another conversation.) Today, we talk about it as a standard. When education is a pursuit, the only goal is to learn more. When we're in a tough conversation, if I seek to understand you, I'm actually pursuing personal growth. By contrast, it's very egocentric for us to think we have all the answers and already know everything we need to know. I don't know your lived experiences. You don't know mine. And the way we find out about those experiences is through interacting and through pursuit.

Even if, on the surface, we appear to hold different beliefs, the more we talk, the more we'll find similarities. Through connection, we can bridge those differences, because our similarities are so strong. If my goal in Compassionate Dialogue™ is to seek to understand you, then I'm broadening my perspective. I won't necessarily change my mind, but I'll gain a level of understanding and empathy that I would not have had if I'd simply focused on your MAGA hat. If I focus on the hat, I can easily decide you're not my kind of person—but is that really true?

WHY NOW?

My sense of urgency in sharing compassionate communication techniques and the RIR Protocol in particular stems from watching the trajectory of our country. With each passing year, we become more and more divided, primarily as a nation but also globally. At the same time, our society as a whole continues to become more diverse. As we interact with more diversity, how can we have compassionate conversations? If we don't figure out how to resolve our differences and divisions, we risk destroying ourselves.

Political correctness has had some harmful effects, but not the ones its critics on the right tend to mention. Rather, I think a consequence of political correctness is that people have stopped talking to each other about issues that matter. Traditionally in polite conversation, you don't talk about religion, race, or politics. However, avoiding those subjects in public doesn't change the fact that they represent significant identities that matter to most of us.

Stifling the conversation makes us more and more isolated, and we don't know what to do because we don't practice having tough conversations. When we do get into them, we don't know how to engage with each other. Big portions of our lives become mysteries to people we care about because we get in the habit of compartmentalizing. Someone wrote to me and said a friend posted a picture of a politician's severed head on her social media, and she told me she was going to unfriend her. I said that approach is part of the problem. She may not change her friend's mind, but it's important to have a conversation about what the post means to her based on the value of that relationship.

The alternative is cancel culture, in which she might cut her friend out of her life without ever telling her why. What's the point? In that scenario, the woman who was angry would continue suffering from her anger, but the canceled friend wouldn't even know she was mad. Having an open conversation, on the other hand, about her perspective and why the behavior is hurtful, could lead to positive change. If it doesn't, then she could say, "I really can't condone that behavior. I wish you the best. I send you blessings, but we can't engage anymore." That conversation offers a mature way to end a relationship, with mutual respect and acknowledgment. It doesn't have to be disrespectful.

Political correctness combined with fear of conflict leads us not to say what we really mean. That lack of conversation doesn't actually change what we believe, though. I lived in Myrtle Beach for six months, and it was very clear who liked me and who didn't. Having been raised in Southern California, I have been weaned on a certain level of fakeness, where people are nice to your face then talk behind your back. But being in the South was actually refreshing; I appreciated not having to guess. People didn't pretend I was okay to my face and then talk about me behind my back or sabotage my efforts.

TRANSFORMING ANGER

I advocate having more open conversations about hard subjects. Calling out has a place, but it's for extreme situations, not everyday interactions. After the riots of January 6, 2021, I wrote a blog post and included pictures. I was calling out the rioters in a productive way. I wanted to invite Americans to look at ourselves and consider who we are and who we want to be. My point wasn't simply to label people as extremists. I do feel that way about them—don't get me wrong. Part of me is angry and frustrated by the response but dwelling in that place doesn't achieve anything positive.

For me, the RIR Protocol takes the anger living inside of me, and instead of letting it eat me up and change me, I make it productive. Transforming it is my responsibility and the essence of the Protocol. The process doesn't prevent the initial anger, disgust, and frustration. The change comes when I choose to interrupt in a way committed to societal betterment. People who commit violence still need to be arrested and face consequences, but the goal is not just punishing the behavior. We also have to heal.

In the case of the Capitol riot, there were instances of some people involved temporarily blocking officers from more violent attacks. Those moments helped spare human life, which is good, but there also has to be accountability. An officer can feel grateful the rioters found their humanity for a moment, but also, what the hell were they doing there in the first place? The RIR Protocol holds space for that complexity, human compassion, anger, and the need for consequences.

We need to hold people accountable, but the way we go about it matters. If we want to climb out of the hole we're in, we have to figure out how to heal the hurt—because everyone who marched in Washington feels hurt, too. I can acknowledge that pain. Whether it's rational or not, I can't diminish that they are hurt. So how do we heal all of our hurt?

Before we get there, let's lay some contextual foundation about the different ways in which we communicate. Once we understand the different styles, we can pinpoint which one we align the most with—and, most importantly, learn how to use that information to enhance our experience using the RIR Protocol.

PAUSE AND PRACTICE

- What is an issue that is unresolved that you have been carrying around with you?

- What do you think is the impact on your body and mind if you continue to carry it?

- What gets in the way of you resolving the issue?

- What would it mean to you to not have to think about it anymore?

CHAPTER 2

WHAT ARE THE DIFFERENT COMMUNICATION STYLES, AND HOW DO WE USE THEM?

Before diving into a solution, it's important to have a foundational understanding of common communication styles and begin to identify where we each fit. I'll offer a framework I believe provides thorough and inclusive definitions of the styles, overlaid with another framework that sheds light on some of the issues we encounter when communicating. It can be difficult to connect when we don't take each other's different styles into consideration.

There are four main types of communicators. It is helpful to understand each one and how they show up in our personal and professional lives so we can adapt accordingly. Because we each process information differently, we can avoid many misunderstandings just by knowing the styles and using tailored strategies to engage with each type of communicator.

ANALYTICAL COMMUNICATORS

Analytical communicators lead with data and are direct. They rely on solid facts for explanation. They avoid emotional validation when thinking. They take a linear approach when communicating with others and convey messages with very specific language. They have the ability to make rational decisions without letting emotions cloud their judgment.

HOW TO COMMUNICATE WITH ANALYTICAL COMMUNICATORS

- Make points using supportive data and facts.
- Be logical.
- Approach them when your ideas are completely formulated.
- Give them time to think it through and form conclusions without pressure.

- When making recommendations, show examples of outcomes for both sides of the argument.
- Answer questions with well-thought-out responses.

INTUITIVE COMMUNICATORS

Intuitive communicators lead with the big picture and are concise. They rely on visuals and like having options. They want to understand the high-level overview and avoid letting details hold them back. They rarely get overwhelmed and make decisions promptly, without overanalyzing specifics.

HOW TO COMMUNICATE WITH INTUITIVE COMMUNICATORS

- Make points from a big-picture context.
- Show a variety of ideas.
- Use visuals to aid discussions.
- Discuss at a high level before going into details.
- Focus on end results rather than intricate processes.

FUNCTIONAL COMMUNICATORS

Functional communicators lead with process and are systematic. They believe in structure and want to understand execution in a step-by-step format. Organization and sequential outlines are essential to avoid mishaps. Details and established practices influence their decision-making.

HOW TO COMMUNICATE WITH FUNCTIONAL COMMUNICATORS

- Address points in a methodical, orderly way.
- Establish a purpose before initiating conversation.
- Focus on processes from start to finish.
- Show project details with timelines and milestones.
- Ask specific questions to create detailed processes.

PERSONAL COMMUNICATORS

Personal communicators lead with emotion and are diplomatic. They value people's thoughts and feelings. They prioritize relationships and establishing rapport at a personal level. They are approachable and are great listeners and advisors. They perceive shifts in people's moods and excel at mediating to resolve conflicts. They make decisions through consultation to consider different perspectives.

HOW TO COMMUNICATE WITH PERSONAL COMMUNICATORS

- Use emotional triggers, such as feeling words, to address points.
- Be authentic and relatable.

- Be a good listener.
- Relate emotions to your thoughts on a topic.
- Show receptivity to different points of view.

KNOW YOURSELF

I am definitely a personal communicator. It is all about the feelings for me first and foremost. I can navigate the other styles but when it comes down to it, I will always want to connect on a personal level whether in my personal life or in business. Moreover, if there is no connection for me, I am usually left wary about getting involved in any way. My way is not the only way, but understanding my style helps me be open to hearing other perspectives. I am also an intuitive communicator and love the "Big Picture," trying very hard *not* to get into the weeds of things. When you put these two together, you begin to get a very clear picture of the way I will typically engage with others. It's all good if we are speaking the same language...but what happens when we aren't?

When I want to shut down or disengage because a different communication style rubs me the wrong way, I have to remind myself to assume positive intentions and remember there *is* more than one way to engage so I can stay present in the conversation. I have also recognized the particular style that triggers me—analytical—and *how* those triggers manifest. This knowledge is invaluable and helps me ask for what I need while honoring the other person's needs, too.

4 Types of Communicators:

Functional	**Analytical**
INTUITIVE	**Personal**

AN INTRODUCTION TO THE FOUR AFFECTS[1]

I now want to overlay the communicator styles described above with another set of four types that relate to our "affect," or more specifically, *how* we express our emotions or feelings—through facial expressions, hand gestures, tone of voice, and other emotional signs, such as laughter or tears. These Four Affects combined with the four communication styles listed above begin to create a fuller picture of who we are as communicators and offer some explanation to why we show up and interpret others the way we do.

---

1   For more information on communication styles, refer to the Four Affects handout in the Appendix.

1. PASSIVE COMMUNICATION

A passive communication style is rooted in a pattern of avoidance—avoidance of expressing needs, opinions, emotions, and so forth. Those who communicate passively, then, often will not speak up when something feels hurtful or otherwise unacceptable, instead allowing those feelings to build up. That build up can lead to an outburst, about which the passive communicator might feel shame or guilt.

2. AGGRESSIVE COMMUNICATION

Those who have an aggressive communication style will express their needs and opinions without regard for those of others, often advocating for themselves to a point that it violates others' rights. Aggressive communicators often interrupt frequently, are quick to criticize or place blame, and speak in a loud, dominating tone of voice.

3. PASSIVE-AGGRESSIVE COMMUNICATION

Passive-aggressive communicators seem passive outwardly but harbor or act on their anger in less obvious ways. This is true even though the object of/reason for that anger can be real or imagined. For example, a passive-aggressive communicator may appear cooperative while behaving destructively behind the scenes, use sarcasm to the max, or deny the existence of a problem when one is clearly there. As a result, passive-aggressive communicators often become alienated from others and feel resentful.

4. ASSERTIVE COMMUNICATION

Those who are assertive communicators advocate for themselves without violating the needs of others, state their feelings and opinions firmly, and are respectful of those around them. Whereas aggressive communicators use "you" statements, assertive communicators use "I" statements. They tend to feel confident, connected, and in control of their own lives and happiness.

4 Types of Affects

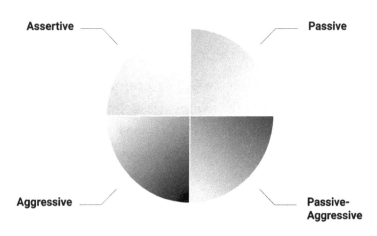

Can you identify your typical affect?

BARRIERS TO COMMUNICATION

These general introductions can get us thinking about the kind of communicator we are. However, before we can apply this information, we also have to identify the barriers that impede our ability to communicate effectively. All communication styles have strengths and challenges that impede connecting.

WHAT GETS IN THE WAY OF HONEST AND DIRECT COMMUNICATION?

I sent out a request to friends and colleagues to ponder the question "Why can't we just talk?" and asked them specifically to address what gets in the way of their having honest and direct communication. Here are some of their responses.

"It takes too much time. I don't want to disappoint anyone, or I just have different priorities and can't be bothered."

—TAYLOR A., SALESPERSON, WHITE MALE

"I often feel like my voice doesn't matter. I often have something unpopular to say and I get tired of being ignored. Also, the gender roles have become more evident recently to me as I work my way up in our organization. The jobs are going to the White males and that limits my ability to be honest because in addition to feeling ignored, I am worried about what I say and how it will be perceived."

—MAITE I., PRINCIPAL, LATINA WOMAN

"When we discuss race as a staff it feels like it's a no-win situation. If I'm silent, I'm not engaged. If I speak up and share my truth, I'm the entitled, privileged White man. Maybe the place to start is sharing that truth?"

—DAVID F., SCHOOL PRINCIPAL, WHITE MALE

"The main reason I would avoid a difficult conversation is that I didn't want to hurt someone's feelings or risk a relationship. But more than that, I would want to be certain that I am not overstepping my boundaries and ensuring I am making an impact in a positive direction as opposed to just sharing my opinion of a matter. Full disclosure: I have difficult conversations often. I've gotten better at them for sure but still don't necessarily like them!"

—LEILAH K., PHD, DIRECTOR OF EQUITY, LCAP, MTSS,
& CATEGORICAL FUNDS, BLACK WOMAN

"Fear of causing the situation to escalate to a place/space that no one is listening to each other. Worried that you could lose a friendship, wording your point of view in a smart enough way that the other person does not shut down and get defensive and dismissive—cause the situation [to] spiral out of control."

—JILL B., SALESPERSON, WHITE WOMAN

"It depends on the audience or parties involved in the conversation. If I'm among friends and family whom I know I can express my true feelings with, it's much easier to have open dialogue. However, if I'm with strangers or acquaintances that I'm unsure of their political/moral/religious beliefs, I'm more hesitant to engage in tough conversations. However, if I find their beliefs are more in line with my own, I have no problem bringing up these discussions. Bottom line, for me it is fear of confrontation when I do not know or am unsure about the person I am talking to."

—SANDRA H., PACIFIC ISLANDER/GUAMANIAN WOMAN

"In this day and age, I feel that people are so tied to their own "right" opinion (and I can be as guilty of this as anyone), that we don't feel like it's even worth it to try to talk to someone. I had this experience when on Facebook someone said something erroneous and demeaning about my religion. I responded very nicely, saying that I would love to talk to this person more about what they had posted because it had not been my experience. I said I'd love to have a discussion about it. Of course, this person was not interested in discussing it, they only wanted to hear things that supported their already-formed opinion."

—WENDY N., BUSINESS OWNER, WHITE WOMAN

"The only thing that gets in the way of having an honest communication is the fear of how the other person will react."

—CLAUDIA B., BLACK WOMAN

"FEAR—of the other person's response—usually expecting them to yell or get crazy. I've found that if I approach people about an issue in a friendly manner, face to face (not by email, phone, text, etc.), it usually has a positive result."

—SANDY P., GRAPHIC DESIGNER, WHITE WOMAN

HOW DIFFERENT STYLES INFLUENCE THE RIR PROTOCOL

The interruption part of the RIR Protocol is easy for me. I'm a natural leader and have always been willing to be both assertive and vulnerable. The RIR Protocol can work for anyone, but some styles—like a more analytical, linear approach—can make the Protocol feel more challenging. First, with this style, feelings are not normally what they want to discuss, and it's harder to lean into the interruption through inquiry when you want to put out data and facts. Understanding how you communicate will help you recognize what challenges you may face when using the RIR Protocol, as well as the strengths you bring to the conversation.

If I were a functional communicator rather than a personal one, my experience could be different. The way the process works depends on how you show up to the conversation. Knowing the four styles lays a foundation for understanding who we are as communicators and what some of the typical obstacles can be.

My approach is all about feelings, and I enter a conversation with how a behavior makes me feel before I get to what I think about it. If you start your statements with "I think," you're coming from a different place. My perspective makes it easier for me to recognize what others feel. People who think first tend to have a harder time recognizing because they're thinking and judging. They'll tend to label a behavior as wrong before they tap into the emotional motivation.

It's tricky to have conversations about charged subjects, in part because these different communication styles come with their own sets of strengths and challenges. If you're the analytical communicator who leads with data and I'm the personal communicator who leads with feelings, we have to figure out how to meet in the middle. If you keep telling me about data and I'm telling you how I feel, we'll talk past each other.

In the school system, when a parent comes in to talk about their child, they are feeling emotional. The principal, on the other hand, will tend to lead with data: "Your child did this." The conversation starts with the behavior and the consequences, but the parent is feeling worried about and protective of their baby. The challenge for the leader is to lead with empathy. To be effective, the principal has to communicate care for the child before issuing a reprimand, even if the child is wrong. Saying the kid is good but had a bad day will make the parent more likely to hear the message than leading with a negative judgment. That subtle shift can change the whole dynamic.

It's important to figure out both what your style is and how to show up for someone with a different style. If I'm analytical but talking to someone who's personal, how can I tap into my feelings more to move the conversation toward the center? We can meet somewhere in the center without sacrificing who we are and still communicate together. How many billions of people are there on this planet? If we can't connect and all coexist together, then we'll destroy each other. I can't even fathom not finding that middle ground.

SUCCESS STORIES

The RIR Protocol might sound good and important in theory, but I guarantee it also works and yields tangible, positive results in practice. Here are just a few of the many success stories.

WORKING THROUGH ISSUES WITH A COLLEAGUE

Many years ago, while working for another equity consultancy, I encountered a difficult colleague who felt I added little-to-no value to the organization. He was in a position of power over me and proceeded to try to make my life as difficult as possible. I initially was stumped by what to do; I hadn't done anything to him and could not figure out why he disliked me so much. In the beginning, I defaulted to some passive *and* aggressive behavior (I'm not perfect) when going to the boss for support, and my initial attempts to work with him failed. At the height of our dysfunction, another colleague and friend overheard him talking badly about me with another coworker. She immediately confronted them both and then let me know what happened. The fact that she was direct reminded me that I had a tool to handle the situation. It was still early on in my personal use of the RIR Protocol, so it was not second nature to me like it is now.

One day, I asked him if I could buy him a coffee (he was addicted to Starbucks) and if we could talk. When he declined the offer on the grounds that a conversation wouldn't solve anything, I reminded him that—at the least—he'd be getting a free cup of coffee. Though the ice was not broken, it was at least cracked enough that he agreed, and we proceeded downstairs to Starbucks. In line, we chit-chatted about family—a natural conversation, especially because his wife had just had a baby.

After we got our coffees and sat down, our conversation turned back to work and the issues at hand. We spoke for several hours, and I was finally able to get to the bottom of his issue with me. Without disclosing too much, he had real and valid concerns. However, those concerns were misdirected at me because he had no outlet for them, and I was the easy target. Afterward, the air between us clearer, we realized we actually could learn to not only tolerate but maybe even *like* one another. That one conversation changed the way we worked together: the climate of hostility was gone in the physical space, and we developed a respectful and healthy way of engaging with one another. The RIR Protocol was truly our savior.

I had always recognized my feelings in this dynamic, but rather than ride my emotional wave, I had let them control me and acted out accordingly. Once I finally took control over them and was able to interrupt through inquiry, we were able to repair and ultimately heal together.

The impact of that moment was immeasurable, as I know it was that interaction that solidified the power and position of the RIR in my life.

CREATING AN EQUITABLE SCHOOL CULTURE

Epoch has been working with one particular district for a couple of years, coaching its equity team. The RIR Protocol has been crucial in providing a foundation for communicating with the members on the team, as well as with the leadership, cabinet, and parents. It's given us a firm foundation that's helpful, as sometimes we have to deal with hostile folks in addition to talking to people who simply don't understand why the work of equity is so important.

When the COVID pandemic started, the school board wanted to be super responsive and immediately roll out computers to all kids within the first week. As they were talking about their plan, though, one of the teachers on the equity team had a visceral response. She said, "We can't do it because all of our kids don't have access. We can give them computers, but if they don't have internet, what good is it?" She was highlighting how the plan would support the families with resources by giving them more, while allowing kids who don't have any to fall further behind.

She says the work around the RIR Protocol gave her the confidence to speak up, even though she was afraid. She felt compelled to point out the mistake she saw the board making and to explain why she couldn't support it. Because the superintendent had also been trained in the RIR Protocol as a part of this equity team, the board members listened to her.

This teacher explained the need for a plan to ensure an equitable rollout of technology that wouldn't inadvertently harm some students. Because of her willingness to step into that difficult place and have that conversation, she single-handedly changed the district's trajectory. The team outlined a plan and the board decided to wait three weeks before sending computers to anyone. In the meantime, they found a partnership with Google to provide mobile hotspots and provide trainings for the rural, agricultural community.

When the computers finally went out, every family in the district had internet access. Some of the parents who already had internet connectivity complained their kids were being held back because of people who didn't have access. However, the district explained it was acting intentionally to take care of everyone rather than deepening the divide, which meant taking three weeks to lay the groundwork for a more equitable plan.

That whole scenario illustrates why we do this work. The RIR Protocol provided a teacher with the skill to recognize what was wrong with the proposal and interrupt by sharing her personal narrative and asking questions. Then, the team repaired the problem by rolling out a solution that worked for everyone. Not only was the experience positive for the individual teacher who spoke up, her action had also a positive impact on all the students, teachers, and administrators in the district. That progress, in turn, starts to build a new climate and culture of recognizing that we're all in this together and only as good as our neighbors.

TALKING WITH FAMILY

After all of our trainings, we do a call to action, inviting people to start small with practicing the RIR Protocol. We ask them to recognize one unresolved issue that's bothering them—one they know they should do something about, however small it might be. Then we ask them to think of one step they could take.

Hundreds of people go out and take the first small step in response. One client talked to me afterward and said she had a personal issue she was struggling with. Her mother is around ninety years old and grew up saying the N-word.

She felt like she wasn't going to change her mother's mind. I suggested instead of trying to change her mind, thinking of a way to interrupt. This client saw her mom as a good person overall, except for this behavior. What could she do to trigger her mother's empathy and bring out a different side of her?

She ended up sharing a story with her mother about one of her students of color. They had a different kind of conversation than usual. That one conversation didn't change her mom's mind, but it was a step toward getting her mom to engage with more positive, realistic, humanizing imagery. That approach exemplifies contact theory—that is, the social principle that states that the more exposure you have to different cultures, the higher your likelihood of engaging with and viewing that culture positively. Opening the door with a low degree of contact, even anecdotal—as we learned in our last example—allows people (like my client's mother) to reflect inward and internalize more positive examples over time.

A major turning point came when her mom said, "You know what, this is just the way I was raised, and maybe it wasn't right." That self-reflection was a huge win. The acknowledgment in itself marked a meaningful shift.

ACHIEVING PROFESSIONAL CLARITY

A friend of mine—we'll call her Sarah—first used the RIR Protocol in a professional capacity. She was tasked with writing a speech for an older man who'd raised two daughters on his own. He was talking about the importance of fathers, but the material he gave her didn't sit right with her. She felt it was very patriarchal and demeaning of women's capabilities.

In the past, before learning the RIR Protocol, Sarah would have ended the professional relationship immediately. Instead, she decided to have a difficult conversation with him, explaining that she'd also been raising two daughters on her own. Sarah explained that his emphasis on men "saving" women felt inaccurate and dismissive of her own experience.

They had a good, long exchange, in which he explained he didn't mean to be dismissive, nor did he believe men were superior or women were incapable on their own. The two were able to have a productive conversation about how to reframe his speech to capture what he actually believed, without alienating his intended audience. Because of the RIR Protocol, she was able to recognize, interrupt, and repair—ultimately having a productive conversation and continuing the work, rather than avoiding and ending the relationship. She showed up, and both sides benefitted.

THE TIME IS NOW

We are at a precipice where we have to decide who we're going to be. I believe we can be amazing, growing and changing with the energy of Aquarius. Or we can spiral down until we no longer recognize ourselves. Part of me honestly feels pity for people who have so much hate in their hearts. What must it feel like to hate all the time? What must it do to a person to be constantly angry? That compassion is my "why." Hatred manifests in our bodies and brings us all down, so the time to act is now.

The other day, a colleague sent me an upsetting text about our budget. I took a deep breath and asked him to call me when he had the time, because it was not a conversation for a text. We had a heated conversation. I was emotionally charged, and so was he. We talked about trust. What was great, though, was my confidence even in the moment that we would come through to the other side. We've been on this journey together, and a difficult conversation would not derail what we've built. In the end, he actually acknowledged to other members of the organization that he'd initially approached me poorly and that my reaction had stirred up fear in him. He also said he appreciated my willingness to speak on the phone with him instead of getting in a texting war. We could have a painful conversation but still communicate and get through it better. I can't imagine living any other way, especially with people I care about.

It's important not to mistake compassion for weakness. Having these conversations doesn't mean you're condoning or consenting to bad behavior. You're simply staying in the relationship and trying to repair a harm.

PAUSE AND PRACTICE

- Re-read the four communication styles. What type of communicator are you?

- Which of the Four Affects do you typically default to?[2]

- How do the two combined impact the way you communicate?

---

2   See Appendix 3 for the Four Affects and communicator style combined handout.

- How do the two combined impact the way you hear others?

- What communication style triggers you the most? How does that show up in your life?

- What are some steps you can take to reduce those triggers and strengthen your communication with the particular style and/or affect?

CHAPTER 3

WHAT IS THE RIR PROTOCOL, AND HOW DO WE USE IT?

When I was teaching in the court schools, my students would come in wearing sagging pants, gang colors, hats, and other items not allowed for their probation. Initially, I fought them on it, telling them to take their hats and colors off. Finally, one of the kids said, "This is survival for us. Imagine me wearing a different color going through my neighborhood. I've got to go through opposing gang neighborhoods just to get to school."

Once I understood that perspective, it shifted me. I acknowledged their need to survive and navigate their world. I wasn't out there with them and unwittingly, I was causing the same harm that had been perpetuated on them while they were in public school...and was the reason they were in alternative education in the first place. I was determined that when they came into my classroom, I would make it a safe place. I started providing clothing they could change into when they got into the classroom. I gave them a secure place to store their belongings. When they came in the room, we were a community...a family.

I was able to set the boundaries of not wearing certain items in the classroom while also recognizing what they needed to do literally to stay alive. I created that environment through listening to my students and empathizing. Had I not negotiated that situation, I would have remained the authoritarian demanding different behavior they couldn't deliver on, getting them suspended, and ultimately getting them reincarcerated for violating their probation.

We set kids up for failure when we don't understand what they have to do to survive. We make blanket rules about not wearing colors, but if they don't wear colors in their communities, they can literally get killed. They're constantly violating their probation, because their probation officers don't take into consideration the reality of their lives. You can't change the behavior you don't like unless you take them out of the environment that endangers them.

Using Compassionate Dialogue™ helped me created a

space where my students could speak in a direct way with me without fear that I would interpret their dissent as disrespect. They were clear that I didn't understand what they were going through, but they were also clear that I sincerely wanted to. Both could be true. I was open to understanding them and meeting them where they were. Together, we collectively took responsibility for our behavior.

Once we made that connection, I didn't have to tell them to take off their hats or colors; they just did it. By the time they sat down for class, they looked like they needed to, with their hats off, pants pulled up, and belts tightened. On the way out, they'd transition back to the appearance they needed outside.

This solution worked for all of us. They got what they needed, and I got what I needed in the space: that's collective responsibility. I wasn't the authority issuing commands. Instead, we collaborated to create boundaries and expectations together regarding how we would behave in the space, together and individually.

RECOGNIZE IT, INTERRUPT IT, AND REPAIR IT

The RIR Protocol is a tool comprising the bigger picture of Compassionate Dialogue™, which is a strategy and a way to engage with others through the lens of compassion. Rather than trying to label someone as wrong, shame them, or prove your point, the goal is to understand one another and then come to a resolution together.

Sometimes that resolution is divorce, but the conversation comes from a place of empathy. Empathy means feeling what it's like to walk in someone else's shoes, which is the level of understanding we're looking for.

Even if I don't agree with what you're saying, how might I empathize enough to understand where you're coming from? This approach is different from sympathy, and definitely different from pity, though people sometimes conflate them. Sympathy means feeling sorry for someone because they had a bad experience, and pity comes from a sense of superiority.

Empathy involves seeing someone eye-to-eye, walking in each other's shoes, and wanting to understand what the other person is experiencing and why they think or feel the way they do. If we can enter dialogue from that empathetic stance, the power dynamic and energy around the conversation shift. A contentious topic may suddenly not be as contentious if both of us share that goal.

The conversations are still hard, but when you come from a place of empathy, they're also purposeful. People aren't simply venting at one another. Both parties feel invested in coming out the other side of that okay. The motivation shifts away from adversarial and toward cooperative. Empathy has compassion, but it maintains strength, too.

USING THE PROTOCOL

The RIR Protocol consists of three steps: recognize it, interrupt it, and repair it. It's a practical skill, tool, or strategy to use, not just a theory.

RECOGNIZE IT

Recognize

Recognition means noticing what a statement, action, or situation makes you feel. You need to see your reaction when a certain feeling is triggered. Then, you can mitigate that reaction. The goal is to stop reacting and start responding. This distinction is critical because your feelings dictate how you make your decisions. Recognizing them puts you back in the driver's seat and allows you to differentiate between your own internal discomfort and the discomfort of a situation.

If anger is triggered in me, I know if I don't ride my emotional wave, then my reaction will be more volatile—and probably not productive. In acknowledging feelings that elicit certain emotions and reactions, I can check them before they come out.

When I then interrupt, instead of reacting and possibly blowing up the situation, I can respond by asking a question. While the other person talks, I can catch my breath and get grounded, allowing me to engage in Compassionate Dialogue™.

INTERRUPT IT

 **Interrupt**

Interruption is intended to stop the behavior or action, but in this case comes from a place of curiosity, while also giving yourself time to figure out how to navigate a complex situation. If a statement is super impactful for you, sometimes it's important simply to share that impact. For example, you could say, "Wow, that really hit me in a weird way. Can you tell me more?" Or you could say, "Wow, that came off wrong. That hurt my feelings. Why would you say that?" By sharing your response and then asking an open-ended question, you give the other person feedback that guides the conversation.

Without training and self-reflection, most people aren't willing to be vulnerable and share when their feelings get hurt. Instead, they blow up, insult the speaker, label the statement stupid, or escalate the situation in some other way. Sharing my feelings is part of the interruption phase because I'm acknowledging the effect on me instead of simply reacting. I'm responding more thoughtfully and then following up with a question.

By sharing the impact, I set the tone for the conversation. I'm not letting the speaker off the hook. I'm being direct by saying, "Wow, where did that come from? That really hurt my feelings. Why would you say that to me?" However, that direct response is different from an uncontrolled reaction. I'm not yelling, "You're just an asshole!" (though I may want to). By exercising compassion, I open space for us to be vulnerable with each other, even with the perpetrator, which is hard to do.

If you think someone is trying to hurt you, it's hard to then bare your neck to them, but doing so shifts the power dynamics. The person already knows their words or actions hurt you, and if you feel compelled to hide that effect, they have power over you. If you're not afraid to share the impact, though, you stay centered in yourself instead of at their mercy. You can speak as equals. I know it sounds counterintuitive but sharing your feelings on your own terms and with strength actually empowers you. It shifts the responsibility back to the other person for trying to hurt you when you call them on it.

The initial interruption sets the tone for everything that follows. How you choose to interrupt determines how difficult the interruption is and how much repair you have to do after.

Strategies for Interruption

As you approach an interruption, remember the following strategies:

- Ask to clarify meaning.
- Ask to understand intent.
- Separate the doer from the deed.
- Address the impact.
- Offer another perspective.
- Connect with empathy.
- Seek to include.
- Acknowledge the speaker.

Stems for Interruption

Consider using some of the following sentence stems as you approach your interruptions:

- "Tell me more about that."
- "I want to understand."

- "What does that mean to you?"
- "What has been your experience with _____?"
- I've had a different experience with _____."
- "I have a different perspective on _____."
- "I think your intention was positive, but what you said felt _____ to me. Can we talk about it more?"
- "I hear your frustration. How do you think we can address that?"

Repair

Repairing is usually an invitation to come back around to the person or the issue and move forward. An interruption can go well, but afterward, people might feel discomfort or find themselves thinking about the conversation and feeling unresolved. If the parties involved don't reconnect, then even if they have a good initial conversation, the experience ultimately separates them.

The repair phase is about what happens a day, week, or month later—or whenever you next engage with the person or issue. What will do you do to heal and move forward?

Sometimes the healing is a particular resolution. Sometimes it's simply reconnecting. If we had a disagreement and I interrupted, then I would reconnect and repair by letting you know we're okay.

If I invite someone out for coffee after we've had a difficult conversation, it will lower their affective filter and signal our relationship is okay. They won't wonder if I'm still mad at them. The repair represents a healing place. The most common strategy we use is engaging. After an interruption, you talk to the other person again and signal you aren't harboring anything against them.

Sometimes repairing needs to go further. If someone makes an offensive statement to me about Muslims, then maybe the repair is for me to come back and say, "You know what? I know that was a hard conversation, but this is why." I could share a story or an article, or I could suggest we do a cultural plunge together and learn more.

Sometimes the repair involves reading. If I'm part of a group with a collective blind spot around Asian culture, then we might do a book study, reading and discussing to bring some of the issues to our consciousness. The repair can be active learning, observation, or experience, but whatever form it takes, it involves engaging with one another.

In many situations, you will be the only person who knows

and is using the RIR Protocol. The other person may not want to engage. They may never give you a chance to repair. You may try and find they're not interested, in which case you'll have to repair on you own, in order to avoid continuing to carry the weight of your response.

In a case where I can't repair collaboratively, I might simply send an email saying, "I'm really sorry we weren't able to resolve this. I know that was a difficult conversation. I wish you the best, and no hard feelings. Take care of yourself." By sending that message, I'm not writing the person off or swearing I'll never speak to them again. I'm essentially giving them a blessing and moving on.

What to Think about When Repairing

As you approach a repair, consider the following strategic questions:

- What boundaries could be developed in order to have a functional, professional relationship with each other?
- What new processes or practices could be implemented?
- What collective learning could happen?
- What support do you need to give for repair?
- How will you follow up and communicate what repair would look like?

Stems for Repairing

Consider using some of the following sentence stems as you approach your repair (when applicable):

- "How about we try to have a fresh start with _____ and be more thoughtful about each other's needs?"
- "It's reasonable that you want _____."
- "You've made a valid point about _____."
- "I'm not sure what the solution to _____ is, but I understand that you're dissatisfied about it. We're a good team. Let's figure out a solution we can both live with."
- "I've taken to heart what you said about _____. I might've seemed defensive, but I was listening and would like to keep talking."
- "I didn't realize what your perspective was before. That's not how I've ever thought about it. I was seeing it completely differently, but now that I know how you see it, I can approach it differently. I might need reminding."
- "I think we went down the rabbit hole about all the issues that have led up to this moment. Can we try to stay present and start with the issue in front of us?"

MAKING AN IMPACT

My first year of college in Arizona, the year I got arrested, I had a friend named Brian. He came from a very segregated area of central Arizona, which had three communities: one predominantly poor and Black, one with wealthy White farmers, and one a mixture of people, including Native Americans. His family lived in the White farming group. Brian and I played volleyball and hung out together. He was my bestie. After months of him talking about me, his family wanted to meet me because he was driving twenty-five miles each way to come see me regularly. They assumed we were dating, though we were just friends.

At the time, I didn't understand that part of the reason why I hadn't met them was because he knew they probably wouldn't like me, due to my race. When he finally brought me home, it was initially one of the most uncomfortable situations ever. However, I was just myself. Even though they had assumptions about who Black people were, they were able to see me as an individual, because they loved their son. I consciously decided to make an impact on the family by continuing to visit and helping them see a different side of Black people that went beyond their limited experiences and stereotypes, one that challenged their assumptions.

Over time, they actually loaned me a vehicle because they thought Brian was driving too much to school and back to bring me to their house. This reduced his commute and made it easier for me to come visit. They saw something different in me, and I also saw something different in them. I didn't agree with their beliefs, but I wanted to make a positive impact by sharing with them who I was as an individual, separate from their stereotypes. My hope was that the next interaction they had with a Black person in their community might yield a different response, a different feeling...a different belief.

I didn't control their behavior or reprogram their beliefs, but I guarantee getting to know me made them think twice about their approach when they were with other Black people. They knew me and how I differed from their stereotypes, which allowed a little room to consider how others could differ, too. For me, that outcome was what I had hoped for. I didn't force a change, but I did feel invested in making an impact. They got to decide what that impact would be for themselves.

I know this approach will irk some people; often the responsibility falls to people of color to help White people see us differently, and many resent having to do this. I truly get it and if I am honest, I often feel the same way. But I am in for the long game and have found that if I keep at it, one person at a time, I can effect change. It may not be a change I will ever see...but my desire is that someone down the road will benefit from my efforts.

Compassionate Dialogue™ makes room to have an impact while also allowing the other person to decide how they'll incorporate it. It's a much cleaner way of interacting than me trying to change you, or you trying to change me. Sometimes we assume if we don't actively try to make a situation "better," if we don't actively fight with someone, then we're condoning their behavior. In fact, by engaging without trying to control, we're actually more likely to make a positive impact.

REPAIR CAN MEAN DIVORCE

If you continue showing up compassionately to conversations but the other person refuses to give as much as they get, then sometimes that relationship is simply not a worthwhile use of your energy. Divorce can be a form of repair *if you've made every attempt* but simply can't find a way for the relationship to move forward. If a team member isn't willing to adjust and becomes the pain point, then the repair may be to remove them from the team or organization. Some employees need to be fired for not doing their job. For example, rather than letting an employee stay who is not effective and has no desire to change, you let them go—that's a repair.

To be very clear here, this is not about merely assimilating a person into the existing climate and culture of an organization, nor is it about being too quick to fire without trying to make reasonable accommodations. As leaders, our job is to create environments where we can work together and our teams can thrive, and that takes effort from all sides.

Through using the RIR Protocol, you're trying to create

a culture and climate collectively. One that ensures the spaces are created for all people, with their unique identities, to not only feel like they belong, but to thrive. If someone continues to resist that culture or climate after multiple interruptions, then you know they do not belong. You go through the steps of repairing, which may mean, in the end, they need to leave the organization. You wouldn't let someone go after the first try, but you also don't want to allow an individual to poison the culture and climate indefinitely.

Using the RIR Protocol, you can come up with a process that supports growth and expansion of thought on both sides. You begin to create processes that are supportive while setting clear expectations and boundaries. Through actively, compassionately engaging and following those processes, you can reach a decision regarding the right time to cut your losses. There is no formula for how these processes can look, so I'll share an example of my own: when I was a faculty member at a university, I had a student with whom I had some challenges. We started off on the wrong foot, and there was an instance where I reacted poorly to something he'd said. I didn't disagree with the point of my message, but I owned that its delivery could have been more compassionate. The student tried to make a complaint to the dean, but the dean had a policy in place: his first question was always "have you spoken to the faculty member yet?" There was a chain of command that was honored, and I was grateful for the opportunity to repair in a way that reinforced clear boundaries and expectations.

Through actively, compassionately engaging and following those processes, you can reach a decision regarding the right time to cut your losses. If you continue interrupting hurtful behavior and they do not understand and alter course, then they're demonstrating that they cannot support the desired culture. On the other hand, be sure to leave room for people to make mistakes. I find that we often leave interruptions one question too soon. If someone says, for example, "I don't care," your next question should be "*Why don't you care?*" That last question can determine intent and make all the difference in your decision.

PRACTICING RECOGNITION WITH THE CONVERSATION STARTER CARDS™

The cards were inspired by clients who repeatedly shared that they needed a tool to support the learning and retention of the RIR Protocol. They explained that they felt very comfortable in session but when they were out in the world, they lost their confidence. That inspired me to create the cards which contain real scenarios they could practice with. Initially, I toyed with the idea of creating them myself but quickly realized that every single person has a story or experience where they "wished they had" done something differently, so why not just go to the proverbial well and collect current examples to build the deck? So, over the course of six months, we collected comments, statements, and stories from real clients and students and used their scenarios to create the first Conversation Starter Cards™ deck. The only requirement for the submission was that the incident, issue, or a statement they either overheard or experienced directly, had to be one they did not respond to either because they were uncomfortable, felt afraid, or didn't know what to do. This was important because the issues you know how to respond to, you will...it is the ones that bring a level of discomfort to you that we need to practice with.

Let's practice with some sample cards. Read the statements below, and start by simply recognizing, at the most basic level, what feelings they stir up for you:

- "There is no White privilege. I grew up poor, and my family worked hard for everything we had."
- "Why are you acting like a girl?"
- "That's gay."
- "You are so articulate."

As you think about your feelings, look at the graphic of the emotions wheel and see if you can notice any additional emotions or nuances about your reaction. To engage effectively, we have to get in touch with our feelings, which can be extremely difficult to do. Our natural instinct is to lash out without stopping to consider, especially if we're used to being in a position of power where we're expected not to show vulnerability.

When we hear something that triggers anger, we tend to skip over recognizing the trigger and the emotion we're feeling and simply react. This is, of course, easier said than done—but it is a muscle you can build. Refer to the example interruption stems earlier in this chapter—those like

"Tell me more about that" and "What does that mean to you?"—to get started.

We'll practice together at the end of the chapter with a specific example.

UNCOVERING THE FEELING

I did an interview with a CEO named Dave Parr regarding a bullying scenario. Normally we try to keep interviews to six-to-seven minutes max, but his was thirteen. We spent roughly ten of those minutes getting to a feeling word. He was in charge of hundreds of people and expected to take action, so he kept jumping to what he wouldn't allow, how he would address the behavior, and immediately interrupting. He wanted to handle the situation, but he was skipping over the essential step of recognizing first.

When he finally got to a feeling, he had an epiphany. He remembered being bullied all through elementary school. His wife didn't even know his story. My spiritual side believes you always get the card you need to get. Once he had the epiphany about his feelings, within thirty seconds he interrupted and repaired like nobody's business. He was used to taking that kind of action, but he had to break through the vulnerable part first.

People who are in high-leverage, C-suite positions of power

and are used to making decisions quickly often struggle with the first step—recognize—in particular. Unless you are accustomed to talking about feelings openly, it might take some time to calibrate how a given statement affects you emotionally before you react. However, it is crucial that you do, because whether you are aware or not, your emotions impact how you interrupt. It is important to know what is your "stuff" and what is not when you are making important decisions.

PAUSE AND PRACTICE

- What feelings did these sample statements trigger in you?

- What would be your typical reaction if you had not used the RIR Protocol?

- If your reaction involved defensiveness or aggression, would it have had the impact you wanted?

- Could there be another way?

- Now that you've identified your feelings, I'm going to invite you to pick one statement and think about how you could interrupt. Here are the four statements again:
  - "There is no White privilege. I grew up poor, and my family worked hard for everything we had."
  - "Why are you acting like a girl?"
  - "That's gay."
  - "You are so articulate."

- Here are the stems again:
  - "Tell me more about that."
  - "I want to understand."
  - "What does that mean to you?"
  - "What has been your experience with _____?"

- "I've had a different experience with _____."
- "I have a different perspective on _____."
- "I think your intention was positive, but what you said felt _____ to me. Can we talk about it more?"
- "I hear your frustration. How do you think we can address that?"

- What did you "Recognize" about your feelings?

- How would/could you "Interrupt"?

CHAPTER 4

HOW DO WE USE COMPASSIONATE DIALOGUE™ INTRAPERSONALLY?

When I met Bonnie, she was a principal in a school district in Northern California. She's a White woman taking real leadership around equity work. She had devoted a significant amount of time shifting the climate and culture of her school toward embedding equity in everything it did. Equity became the way they did business instead of an isolated initiative.

Her story has inter- and intrapersonal components. She attended a funeral with her mom, and afterward, they were sitting at a table together during the reception. A Black man, who was a friend of the family and also at the funeral, approached their table. He introduced himself and expressed his condolences. After he left, her mother essentially asked who "that Black man" was and why he would visit their table.

Bonnie said the comments stirred up old feelings for her. Her mom grew up in a more overtly racist era, but she's also a fundamentally good person. Bonnie has struggled with that disconnect. She's never thought her mom's behaviors or comments around race were okay, but she also never knew how to interrupt them. She blamed herself and felt like a coward for not speaking up, but it's hard to know how to interrupt your own mother. I understand the bind. I often don't know how to interact with my mom, because there is always something that YOUR mom can and will do that drives you crazy...no matter how well you have mastered the RIR Protocol.

So, what can we do when we find ourselves wrestling with the disconnect between our values and actions?

ADDRESSING INTERNAL STRUGGLES

The RIR Protocol works in three spheres: *intra*personal, where you look inside; *inter*personal, where you work with other people; and then organizational or systemic. The beauty of the RIR Protocol is once you've mastered it, you can use it in all aspects of your life. The recognize, interrupt, and repair steps are the same, regardless of context. Recognition involves noticing the feeling, whether toward our own behavior, toward a trigger from another person, or about a system or policy. That feeling calls us to action.

Intrapersonal Compassionate Dialogue™ represents self-improvement. How do I work on myself to recognize the behaviors or beliefs that don't resonate with who I think I am? How can I make my actions more congruent with who I say I am? Intrapersonal RIR helps us navigate those conflicting spaces. For instance, someone might say they're very liberal, accept people for who they are, and don't see color—but then when a Black person is standing on the corner, they lock their doors. That behavior is not about the Black person or even some unstated beliefs; it represents what the self-described liberal person has internalized compared to what they say externally and believe about themselves.

When you come face to face with these kinds of internal, intrapersonal contradictions, you can use the RIR Protocol to unpack and begin to rectify them. These incongruencies may be conscious or unconscious. Either way, they're deeply embedded.

Sometimes the conflict stems from a religious upbringing that doesn't align with personal beliefs. For instance, maybe a young woman grew up Christian and she believes sex, according to the Bible, is only for procreation. At the same time, she has sexual feelings she wants to explore. Every time she masturbates, though, she feels guilty and she thinks she's going to hell. That situation poses an internal conflict. She received the religious beliefs from others; she wasn't born believing self-pleasure was a sin. However, that lesson creates a conflict between feelings and beliefs.

If you're fine with the beliefs you've learned and they don't create an internal struggle, then there's no problem. Even if other people don't agree with your belief, as long as you feel in harmony with it and yourself, then you're okay. However, if your received beliefs and your internal values about right and wrong conflict, then there's work to do. The RIR Protocol only comes into play when you need to address conflict.

We need to look at ourselves objectively and admit when we're in that struggle, which may stir up some measure of shame. The first step is recognizing. When you recognize an internal conflict, the RIR Protocol then asks what feelings it brings up for you. Does it bring up shame? Does it bring up anger, sadness, or frustration? You have to be willing to look at yourself. What discomfort does the internal conflict cause in you? If it causes you shame, you may have a harder time addressing it, because you'll feel you can't be as open about it as if you were feeling fear, for example.

It's important to understand the feeling associated with the behavior or belief, because that feeling determines your level of comfort moving forward. The outcome might not ultimately be feeling comfortable, but we want to get out of our own way. Otherwise, we'll find ourselves in denial because we don't want to address the issue. If we recognize that tendency toward denial, we can interrupt and move beyond it.

INTERNAL DIALOGUE

The intrapersonal process takes the form of an internal dialogue with yourself. The RIR Protocol harnesses our innate abilities to use healthy communication skills to engage in conflict. I didn't invent something new so much as pay attention to normal, productive strategies and articulate them.

Before the Protocol was even the Protocol, I used the RIR growing up. My mom was mostly absent from my life because she was working and traveled as a singer. She went to Vietnam with the United Service Organization (USO). She lived in Las Vegas and was a resident artist at the Flamingo Hotel. My siblings and I had contact with her, but she was rarely at home. Our grandmother was our consistent adult and raised us.

When I was eleven, my mom went to Europe and essentially never came back. She gave my twin sister and me the option to come join her, because we were the youngest. However, we said no, because even as pre-teens, moving to Europe with our mother who was never around seemed ridiculous. We were happy in our home and in our community, which was very accepting of all people. Then, when we were twelve, my grandmother had a stroke. That essentially changed all of our lives. She could no longer care for us, and we had to start working.

We had a family meeting with my three older brothers, who were seventeen, eighteen, and nineteen at the time. We talked about what needed to happen in order to prevent Child Protective Services from taking us away. We discussed the fact that my sister and I needed to work, because our brothers could not support us and the household. We needed to get jobs. My saving grace was that I was tall—I was already at least 5'8" and 135 pounds at eleven years old. I looked like a late teen, old enough to have employment.

Getting a job marked the beginning of my lying. I wasn't a liar before and lying didn't come naturally to me. Still, I had to lie to get the job and then again when I missed school. I had to start forging my grandmother

s name, because there were no adults in the house to write me a permission slip to get back into school if I overslept or didn't feel well. Over time, lying became a part of who

I was, first out of necessity and then later, through habit. I'd exaggerate to impress my friends or cover up what was actually going on in my family.

The plan with my siblings worked. We kept the family together. My sister and I found our way into sports and realized it would give us a ticket out of our situation. We both got full athletic scholarships. She played basketball for UCLA, and I played volleyball at United States International University in San Diego. By the time I got into my twenties, though, I was lying about things I didn't really have to lie about. I'd simply become a liar. That situation truly presented an internal conflict. I distinguished between what I would consider a necessary lie and an unnecessary lie. I had no guilt lying about my age to survive, but I struggled with my tendency to lie to make myself seem better. It was unnecessary and didn't have a positive impact on my life.

I'd catch myself in unnecessary lies and feel upset, ashamed, and angry. I'd ask myself, "Why did you do that?" Once I started to pay attention to the behaviors, I recognized what was coming up for me and began to interrupt. I hadn't developed the RIR Protocol yet, but the process came naturally for me. I made an agreement with myself that the next time I lied unnecessarily, I would own it and tell the person I'd lied to or otherwise make the situation right.

The universe is magical, because I had the opportunity

to put this agreement into practice almost immediately. I would play in a beach volleyball draw tournament in Mexico every year; a draw tournament means your partner is randomly drawn out of a hat and you do not discover who you are playing with until the day of the match. It is literally the luck of the draw: sometimes you are lucky, and sometimes you are not. You sign up, provide your ranking skill level, and then get matched. I actually love draw format; it helps keep my competitive edge from consuming me and allows me to enjoy the sport differently. But this year I was attending with a former college teammate who I hadn't seen in years. At a draw tournament, you don't see the people you attend with unless you're matched. It is simply too big of a tournament and with the conflicting schedules, it is almost impossible to connect for more than a few minutes. Since I really wanted to spend time with my former teammate and her family, I lied to get us paired together.

I made up a completely fake, lame-ass excuse for the organizer regarding why my friend and I had to be partners, just to get my way. There was no truth to anything I said. When I hung up the phone with her, I literally hung my head down and cried. Even as I was lying to her, I could not stop myself and ultimately, I felt ashamed when it was all said and done. Internally, I felt (and still feel) lying was not okay. I didn't want to manipulate people to get my way, but I also didn't seem to know how to stop. At the time, I did not have the courage to call her back, so instead, I decided to mail a check with a long letter explaining why I'd lied, sharing what I did not have the courage to say to her face. I apologized. Remembering the experience still makes me emotional. I was completely intimidated and honestly petrified to see her after having confessed to lying to her.

When I saw her, though, she gave me a big hug and thanked me. She said she understood why I'd lied and knew it had taken courage to come clean. She said people lied to her all the time, but I was different in that I admitted what I'd done and made it right. I thanked her for forgiving me.

It was such a painful process that I completely stopped lying after that incident. My interruption was an agreement with myself that if I ever lied again for an unnecessary reason, I'd have to own it. I didn't ever want to go through that experience again, so I quit cold turkey. Stopping lying was my repair. I realized as long as I held myself accountable, I was true to my word. Once I gave my word to myself, I kept it and stopped lying overnight.

To this day, I'd say I don't lie. If I find myself exaggerating, I try to own it and correct myself in the moment. With the RIR lens, I understand why my internal agreement keeps me honest. Thirty-five years later, I still follow the same rule of owning through recognizing, interrupting, and repairing any unnecessary untruth.

It takes self-accountability and self-discipline to walk through this process in your own mind. At the end of the day, you're answering to yourself. Had I not spoken up, the organizer never would have known, or she might have suspected and lumped me in with the other people who lied to her. The RIR Protocol, though, offers a way not only to interrupt behaviors but also to deepen relationships, with yourself and others. I started the work intrapersonally, but my interruption and repair also deepened the relationship with someone whose opinion I cared about. We didn't become best friends, but we palpably raised the level of respect between us.

MAKING TOUGH DECISIONS

In trainings, we talk about intrapersonal RIR when facing tough decisions around shifting beliefs and behaviors. Shifting a behavior might come into play when you recognize you're drinking too much, for example, which stirs up negative feelings the next morning. Your interruption may start with deciding to drink only on the weekends. I made that decision when I found myself socially drinking most nights with my husband, not heavily, but enough that I felt groggy. I recognized that I didn't like the habit and interrupted it. I asked my husband not to open bottles of wine on weeknights; if he wanted to drink, he could just have a whisky. Asking him for support was part of my application of the RIR Protocol, incorporating an interpersonal action to help reach my intrapersonal goals.

Sometimes we need our friends and family to help keep us accountable. When people want to lose weight, they often get a trainer for accountability. If I pay a trainer rather than simply starting a gym membership, I'm more likely to show up. So, if you find yourself facing a tough intrapersonal decision, consider whether there are interpersonal resources you can enlist to ensure your success.

If you feel called to start deepening your own recognition and then interrupting and repairing your internal conflicts, you might start by asking yourself whether there's a personal decision you've been struggling to make. Which issues are you avoiding or minimizing? My philosophy around conflict and making decisions is that you know something is unresolved if you're still thinking about it. If I have an extremely difficult interaction with someone but don't keep revisiting it, then the impact is gone. On the other hand, if I find myself fixated on issues from long ago, then they're still unresolved for me.

An issue can be resolved, no matter how hard it is. An issue that keeps lingering in your mind weeks or years later is unresolved, no matter how simple it might seem on the surface. The continued thoughts indicate you're still processing and need some form of repair.

Maybe you wish you had acted or spoken differently. I was once in a bar and talking to a guy I was interested in, but he was there with another woman who was a friend. I asked him if he wanted to dance, and he said, "Well, I've got my friend." In front of her, I asked, "*Her?*" It was really demeaning, and I didn't mean it exactly the way it came out. The minute I said it, though, he put his arm around her to comfort her. I could tell I'd hurt her and made myself look like an ass. I regret that incident, but the only repair I can do now is within myself. I was nineteen years old and will never see those people again. It was a formative moment for me, though, because it forced me to pay better attention to my language.

Now, when I notice I've said something hurtful, regardless of my intent, I interrupt and repair it immediately. I'll say something like "You know what? I see you're having a reaction to what I said, and I want to clarify what I meant. It came out wrong." I can't repair what I said to that young woman so many years ago, but I can ensure I don't act that way in the future. Intrapersonal work stems from those incidents you can't let go of, even decades later.

If you're still thinking about something, it's unresolved and therefore fair game for intrapersonal RIR.

INSIDE-OUT APPROACH

I did a cultural plunge with a friend of mine, a White English man in his mid-fifties. I asked him questions about culture, and I've known him since I was twenty-one. I would say that when it comes to racial issues, he's very aware—maybe not fully versed, but has a deep passion and understanding of the topic. He grew up and went to school with diverse friends. He's dated women from various ethnic backgrounds. He is truly a good guy. However, I asked him to define his culture, and he couldn't. He talked about what his culture was not, but he couldn't talk about what it *was*.

My epiphany in that moment was: here's a very "woke" White guy (I put this in quotes because I am not a huge fan of the term but in this moment, it conveys my meaning), who I would have thought could talk about what it means to *be* a White guy and what his culture looks like, but he could not. We talked, and he said he'd never thought about some of what I was bringing up. He said he'd have to think about it, which I know he will.

People of color think about their culture all the time and do not typically have trouble identifying its characteristics. White folks are usually the ones who struggle, whether because of guilt or simply never considering the question. When I think of this dynamic, I always come back to the water the fish swims in: the fish is surrounded by it, so it cannot see it for what it is.

If you're reading this book, you're likely already a reflective practitioner. You may already be awake, engaging comfortably with people different from you, and seeking out diversity. You're probably a kind, wonderful person—and you may still have blind spots. So, what happens when you face someone who's actually resistant, doesn't believe White privilege or inequity exists, and thinks immigrants are taking their jobs?

There are many barriers to self-reflection, from denial to righteousness. No matter where you are on the continuum, there are opportunities to reflect and go deeper with this work.

Equity work in general often fails to reach its full potential because it tends to focus externally on those who are most marginalized. It centers on how to "fix" them or fix a system. By contrast, at Epoch, we use what we call an inside-out approach. We ask people to look at who they are and how who they are impacts the relationships, climate, culture, and systems in place. I have often found people who are extremely "awake" and doing the work are very rarely asked to look at their own role in perpetuating the inequities.

In addition to looking at yourself and your own culture, ask yourself about the beliefs you were raised with and which ones are contrary to who you think you are. Of all the identities you have, which ones bring you joy? Which ones have you had to alter the most? Which one has been the most consistent over your lifetime? Which one creates the greatest risk to you? And which one brings you the greatest safety? Examining yourself and your identity in this way can take you to a place you may never have gone before.

Personally, the identity of greatest risk for me is my skin color. We are born with identities we have to own and navigate in our lives. We may feel the need to hide them, abandon them, or deny them, depending on the space we're in. My context can determine whether or not I can show up fully as myself. When I think about the intrapersonal, that identity is part of my struggle. There's a conflict between, "I'm a proud Black woman" and "I can't be as proud here." If I show up too proud, then I am uppity, aggressive, or an "angry Black woman," which plays into stereotypes that could cause me to be unsafe.

In considering identity at an Epoch workshop, one White woman said she'd never thought of people having to alter who they were. She just gets to show up. A Latina woman responded by saying it had never occurred to her that people *didn't* have to alter who they were. It was not a moment of confrontation but rather a moment of clarity, which is the beauty of using the RIR Protocol. Both women had signed on to creating a space of inquiry rather than judgment. In the process, they saw how we bring our own perspectives, and it's important to cultivate the understanding that our experience is not everyone's experience. Even if some of the realizations come from a place of being naïve, we have to articulate them before we can act on them.

When we face these questions about our own identity and gain clarity, we open the door to more fully understanding other people's identities. We can work from the inside out. Even if we weren't consciously ignoring other identities before, asking these questions gives us a better lens for engaging with others in an empathetic and equitable way. The more self-reflective we become and the more we understand ourselves, the more empathy we're able to have for other people.

Using Compassionate Dialogue™ creates a space where we can be vulnerable to muse and say what we're thinking, without worrying about getting it wrong. We can be honest without blocking ourselves through guilt and shame. Compassionate Dialogue™ calls for us to engage authentically and thoughtfully, to be vulnerable throughout the process; and it is in engaging from that place that we are able to extend grace for ourselves and others.

SPEAKING UP

Bonnie struggled for years about how and whether to intervene regarding her mom's racist comments. By the time of the funeral, though, she'd been living the RIR Protocol. She saw the opportunity to lean into the internal dissonance she felt regarding not being able to interrupt her mother on these issues. She found her motivation because her mother made these particular comments in front of children at their table. She recognized she had to do something, because otherwise she was allowing her mother to perpetuate racism in the next generation.

She shared with her mom how the comment made her feel and asked why it mattered what color the man was. She said she wanted help in understanding where that comment came from. Without the RIR, she would have let it go like she always had. Instead, by recognizing her feelings and experiencing a call to action because of the spectators, she interrupted. Afterward, she thought doing so in a public place was not the most effective tactic, but she was at least glad she had started. It made addressing the "next time" an easier task to consider, and she then committed to figuring out how to interrupt in a gentler way. She could refine her approach while continuing to act.

The intrapersonal piece flowed from a long-term internal conflict and confusion about how to engage her mother in a meaningful way. Because children were involved, she could not let it go. That intrapersonal step became interpersonal when she engaged her mother and tried to deepen the understanding between them. She ultimately interrupted and repaired on both levels.

The interaction didn't change her mother's behavior, but her repair was to continue trying to support her mother in understanding why her comments were harmful. The intrapersonal repair was her new commitment to interrupting and engaging, rather than avoiding or staying stuck.

PAUSE AND PRACTICE

- Of all the identities you have, which ones bring you joy?

- Which ones have you had to alter the most?

- Which one has been the most consistent over your lifetime?

- Which one creates the greatest risk to you?

- Which one brings you the greatest safety?

CHAPTER 5

HOW DO WE USE COMPASSIONATE DIALOGUE™ INTERPERSONALLY?

Rochelle is an instructional specialist at a district in which she specifically focuses on supporting marginalized populations: African Americans, English language learners, and first-generation college students whose families have not been to college and don't know how to support that process. So rather than directly teaching a class, her team helps provide these groups with supports to make them college ready, like a specialized counseling service.

A prior chief academic officer (CAO) had done a review

of programming and determined a grant-funded program supporting Rochelle's target populations wasn't yielding enough on the investment, so they decided to cancel the program. In doing so, however, they didn't consult with anybody the program impacted. It was simply a book-balancing measure as opposed to the result of critically examining the situation and determining whether they could improve the outcomes.

When a new CAO came on board, who happened to be a Black woman, Rochelle talked to her about the issue. The CAO also agreed the cancellation was problematic and the program actually did have long-term, qualitative benefits no one had considered in purely looking at the costs. She understood the fiscal responsibility piece but thought a better approach would be to make changes rather than scrapping the program entirely. She and Rochelle wanted to enter into a new conversation.

At that point, Rochelle's director accused her of having a "Black agenda," meaning favoritism or nepotism toward African Americans. The director pointed to the equity team, which had Black people on it; the fact that the new CAO was Black; and the fact that Rochelle is Black and was focused on getting back a program for Black children. Rochelle sat with this comment, and it made her angry.

The idea of a "Black agenda" is not new. People accused

President Obama of the same thing. Does that mean every other White president had a White agenda? Yes, actually, but that fact is beside the point. The implication is that, somehow, White people are above any scrutiny, because they offer the great "White hope," insinuating that because they're there to save the day, their actions are wholesome and neutral. Supposedly they think about everyone, but a person of color in power will only have a narrow racial agenda, which could deprive White people. These critics tend not to flip the lens and wonder what happens when a White person is in charge. This lack of reflection continues to minimize what a person of color in power is able to contribute. It also further diminishes the gifts and perspectives diverse backgrounds can bring and at a base level, it perpetuates the deficit mindset regarding ability that constantly follows people of color.

Rochelle found herself in a dilemma. She felt she had no choice but to speak up. She needed to call out the double standard in which no one questions whether a group of White people can make unbiased decisions about a whole student body, including children of color. Still, she felt very scared because she was talking to her superior.

POWER DYNAMICS

The interpersonal involves how we communicate with each other, whether our supervisors, partners, spouses, friends, or colleagues. The RIR Protocol is not about changing other people. Rather, it offers a guide for interacting. If I'm truly practicing the RIR Protocol, I can't attach its value to your response or reaction. It's about aligning with my own values and choosing how to engage.

The RIR Protocol helps us navigate the external dynamics that can get in the way of our ability to communicate effectively with each other. Using the RIR Protocol supersedes power dynamics and allows me, for example, to engage with a boss from a grounded space rather than a reactionary one. It levels the playing field for our ability to engage with each other from a place of compassion.

Often when power dynamics are in play, people lose their ability to communicate effectively. They feel fear or a sense of inadequacy. Because the RIR Protocol centers on its user and not the other person, though, it allows us to say and do what we need to. We may still feel fear, but we'll be grounded in ourselves.

When I speak using the RIR Protocol, I know *why* I need to communicate as opposed to simply reacting. When I choose to engage with my supervisor or another authority figure, I have a sense of purpose. I feel morally compelled to speak up, with an internally rather than externally generated motivation. If someone speaks to me, I can choose whether to engage. If I choose to engage and use the RIR Protocol, then I get to engage on my terms.

Having a motivation stemming from my own values also helps supersede my fear. I may be afraid to speak up to my colleague, but if a child is in danger, for example, I will do what I need to do because my need to care for that child supersedes the fear of engaging with my colleague. I have to act. Compassionate Dialogue™ helps us see our triggers as calls to action. If we're clear on what the trigger is, why it triggers us, and what that feeling state means to us based on our values and beliefs, then we can overcome potential barriers to communication, even if we're in a subordinate position within an organization.

BEING UNDERSTOOD

Using the RIR Protocol means entering discussions wanting to be understood, not wanting to be right, which can be difficult. It's hard to say what you need to say and then move on, independent of the other person's reaction. Human nature and societal norms are such that when someone triggers us, it's tempting to try to make them wrong and shame them. We want to blame them. We want them to apologize. All these wants are external, though. The RIR Protocol shifts my focus and leads me to practice understanding and connecting with the other person, instead of making them wrong.

If someone triggers you, the RIR Protocol certainly doesn't stop you from feeling pissed off, but it does help you let the experience flow and then let it go. When you come from a place of inquiry, you have more time to catch your breath. You give the other person the opportunity to explain, in case there was some kind of misunderstanding. Simply clarifying whether you heard and understood the other person correctly establishes a pause and a layer of connection rather than launching into telling them off. Everyone has the chance to get on the same page.

A significant number of negative interactions simply stem from misunderstandings. If we can suspend judgment, or at least hold it back even for a minute and ask for clarity, we might realize we're actually talking about different issues. I've had many experiences of reacting because I thought I heard something hurtful, only to find the other person didn't mean what I thought they did. I've also been on the receiving end of negative interactions when people misunderstood me. We were actually expressing the same idea in different ways, but they misinterpreted my intent and reacted before clarifying. My twin sister and I do this ALL THE TIME!

Coming from a place of inquiry is particularly important in interpersonal relationships because the RIR Protocol asks you to choose grace over anger—which is much easier said than done. However, it's rewarding, because you're choosing grace not just for the other person but also for yourself. You don't succumb to the reactionary emotion.

Compassion is for all of us—others and ourselves. We can allow ourselves the beauty and strength of engaging compassionately, by not punishing ourselves for our feelings. We acknowledge them, address them, and then move past them. When we feel triggered, we don't have to repress our feelings—doing so only causes us to blow up later, because we don't have a healthy outlet for them.

MODELING EFFECTIVE COMMUNICATION

Interpersonal skills don't just apply to one-on-one situations. They also help with group dynamics. The underlying Protocol is exactly the same. I can use it as an individual interacting with all kinds of people who have no idea what it is. Through my example, they can learn to engage and communicate more effectively, by seeing the way I engage. I shape the conditions of our interactions with each other.

If I come from a place of feeling triggered by someone and thinking they want to hurt me, I can choose to get curious and bring some grace to the interaction. I can ask what they really meant and whether they're intentionally trying to get a reaction from me. The inquiry can be quite direct and shift the energy from me feeling attacked to the other person needing to explain.

If someone triggers you, it's important to practice changing your triggers—because you can't change a person. If you try to trigger me, using the RIR Protocol helps me refuse to take the bait; then you won't get to me. Every time you attack me, I'll come back with inquiry. My repair may be clarity that we don't see eye-to-eye, so bless you, but there's no reason to have further conversations. I maintain control over my own well-being.

I can influence how others communicate by showing up in the RIR Protocol myself. If everyone in a group knows the Protocol, though, then we can all speak the same language, and our community communication becomes even more effective. In that situation, we all come from a place of inquiry. There are fewer accusations and attacks. There's less need for defensiveness because everyone's working on themselves.

The RIR Protocol is hugely helpful with regard to power dynamics in groups, because there are so many different roles and variables than there are in a one-on-one interaction. It also encourages healthier interactions because the people in charge use the same approach. As a result, they're also entering the conversation not from a place of needing to control but from a place of inquiry, which is empowering. Effective leaders model effective communication.

BEING A BETTER FRIEND

One example of interpersonal RIR comes from a longtime

friend of mine. We started off playing volleyball together, and from there, we began hanging out socially. She's a great person, but she also tended to have a "grass is always greener" mindset. We'd make plans, and then she'd cancel at the last minute because something better came up, even if it meant leaving friends in the lurch with concert tickets. She also wasn't direct about saying she didn't want to go; instead, she'd make an excuse, implying I or other friends had done something wrong.

As this pattern became clear to me, I knew I needed to do something about it but was not sure what. Intuitively, I felt this friend and I had some spiritual work to do together. But it was getting increasingly harder to stay in relationship with her. She had wonderful qualities, but at the end of the day, she usually left me feeling bad and like I wasn't important enough.

The last straw happened on New Year's Eve. I'd planned an intimate evening with a few friends to create vision boards together. At first, this friend seemed unsure, and I told her to let me know. Then she said yes, she was in and would bring a few things. I proceeded with making the plans and getting everything ready. The night of the party, my other friends showed up early with food, even though they were only supposed to bring themselves. I asked what was going on, and they said they'd been playing volleyball with the other friend earlier, and she'd been badmouthing me, saying she didn't want to go to the party, but I'd pressured her.

My other friends knew what she said wasn't true. In fact, they'd had their own experiences of her backing out on commitments with them. So, they showed up early and brought the food because they had a feeling she wasn't going to show up and knew I was depending on her contribution; basically, they didn't want to leave me hanging. The situation brought me to tears, but not for the reason you might be thinking. The friend who'd let me down elicited anger and a resolution in me that this would be the last time. What brought me to tears was the act of love, kindness, and support from those friends who showed up to interrupt the situation, in their own way. They knew there was something they could do to help make it right, and they acted without asking if it was necessary. They saw a need, and they responded.

As it turned out, the other friend did show up, and at that point, I was furious with her. She was loudly taking phone calls in another room and saying she didn't know how long she'd *have* to stay at the party. Finally, I said, "You can leave, hon. You don't have to be here if you don't want to be." She said she wanted to stay, so I dropped it. I decided I wanted to be present for the rest of the evening and not let the situation ruin my New Year's.

The next day, I was having a garage sale, because I was

selling my house and moving to England. This same friend showed up to help. Earlier, I'd suggested we could hang out, but given everything that had happened, I asked her why she was even there. It seemed like she knew she'd messed up. In that moment I knew it was time for us to part ways. I sat her down on the couch and proceeded to "break up" with her. We were both in tears. I explained that I loved her, but she'd hurt me and embarrassed me, and I didn't want people in my life who could treat me that way.

The RIR Protocol began internally, because I recognized I didn't need her in my life; that she was detrimental to the life I wanted to have. I needed to interrupt the behavior and move on. Unlike many people today who ghost each other, though, I took the time to tell her. We sat there together and cried. She stayed with me all day and thought that doing so would change my decision—but for me, our relationship was over. I told her I loved her and wished her the best, but I was choosing differently for my life. I realized if we had any more spiritual work to do together, it would have to happen in heaven. I had no more space or energy for it here.

Once I had my own internal clarity, I could communicate with her about exactly how I felt and what I planned to do. It turned out (to my dismay) that I couldn't completely cut her out; I quickly realized how deeply embedded she had become in my life. We were in a book club, on a volleyball team, and on a softball team together. We saw each other three or four times a week, and she kept trying to make closer contact. I remained polite toward her, but I was clear about my own needs and values and thus stayed away.

In the end, through that behavioral modeling, she came to respect my boundaries. I was clear without engaging in a power struggle, which influenced her. She "courted" me for six months, and finally, I saw she was really changing. I could have stuck to my guns and said, "You're out of my life forever because you don't know how to treat me right, and I have made my decision." Instead, I allowed there to be grace for her to see the situation, reflect on herself, and grow into someone better, which is ultimately what happened.

She's now one of my closest friends, but only through that process. We had the hard discussion in 2007 and were it not for the RIR Protocol, we would not be talking today. Instead, our relationship is deeper, more real, and more mutually respectful. She grew as a person, which influenced her relationship with others as well. The issue was with her behavior, not her as a person. My interruption helped put her on a course of self-development and self-reflection that made her a better friend to all of us.

Even if we hadn't found that happy ending, the process would have been worth it. I was not attached to her coming back in my life. In fact, I was clear that I was parting ways.

At the same time, I remained open because we all make mistakes in our life. If people didn't forgive me for my mistakes, I'd have far fewer friends. The RIR Protocol offers grace instead of personal blame, shame, or punishment.

Everyone is on their own journey and has their own baggage that they bring to the table. When we can start to clear that baggage consciously, we show up as better people for ourselves and for our families, friends, colleagues, and communities. We have to make room for people to grow. We can recognize when people become better, which is a hope I hold for everyone. Imagine how different the world would be if we all took that approach.

INTERRUPTING STEREOTYPES

Elsa is a Mexican woman I initially met while consulting together on behalf of separate organizations for a project with a large school district in Northern California. She is very smart, passionate, professional, and precise. She always forced people to challenge their own stereotypes, and I loved working with her.

In addition to being a consultant, she was also a teacher at the time that I met her. However, shortly after, she decided to pursue a superintendency position. This is significant and a testament to her brilliance because she got hired as a superintendent without a doctoral degree in a predominately White, somewhat bigoted agricultural community outside of San Diego. The district had a large Latino population, and she was able to bring her passion for ensuring kids of color have access to academic rigor regardless of the barriers they attempted to erect. She knows we don't do kids any favors by making work easy or feeling sorry for them. We need to give them rigor with social supports to ensure their success. Research[3] has shown that if we spent more time on the social supports along with the rigor, student achievement would surpass annual grade level expectations.

Social supports are defined as:

- Strong social **relationships** among students and adults **in and out of school.**
- Relationships imbued with a sense of **trust, confidence,** and **psychological safety.**
- Opportunities for students to **take risk, admit errors, ask for help, and experience failure** along the way to higher levels of learning.

Soon after Elsa was hired, a classified leader who had been on her interview panel told her, "Don't make me regret hiring you." She also indicated that Elsa had only been

---

3   Lisa Delpit, *"Multiplication Is for White People": Raising Expectations for Other People's Children* (New York: The New Press, 2014).

hired because the board wanted a Latina. In that narrative, she simply checked a box.

Looking at her in relation to a quota doesn't acknowledge her individual brilliance and truly badass qualities, the energy she brings, or her excellence—only her race. That framing minimized her expertise and made her feel expendable. It sounded like any other Brown or Black person could take her place, regardless of her particular potential and impact. The conversation is an old and tired one at this point—about affirmative action and how people of color cannot possibly be qualified for high-level positions (and thus the bar must be lowered to include them), and their performance will be subpar because of it. So much to unpack here, but that is for another book.

Anyway, back to Elsa. Because of the way she'd grown up, she'd already internalized some negative stereotypes that made her feel less-than. In her family, she didn't have many examples of women being front and center. She felt susceptible to doubting whether she belonged and was qualified enough and wondering whether critics were right that Black and Brown candidates were getting special treatment.

The new position made her come to grips with who she is, who she believes she is, and who other people believe she is. How could she reconcile all those different visions and versions of herself?

My friend Eddie says identity is like a shopping cart. People put shit into your shopping cart from the day you're born. It starts filling up with your family values and beliefs passed down. As you become more conscious, you add your own values and beliefs, so who your family says you are and who you say you are as an individual may differ. At school, teachers add their own ideas, whether they tell you you're smart, you talk too much, or you should be an actor or an athlete. Putting shit in your shopping cart. Everywhere you go, people add their own judgments and stereotypes to your cart. You end up adapting to some of them, and others you just keep carrying around, even if they don't necessarily resonate with you.

In Elsa's case, she felt the dissonance between who she knew she was and who the board member thought she was. At that point, Elsa not only knew the RIR Protocol but had also taught it to others, so she fully embodied it in her life. She recognized feeling very hurt, because her family had made so many sacrifices to allow her to become an educational leader. Her children had to change in the school bathroom for prom because they lived so far from their school. It also meant that her husband had to make a long commute to get to work and to support the kids. So, the implication that her only value to the district, after so much hard work and sacrifice, was in her race and gender—not her skills and excellence—just broke her heart.

In order to help herself not be hijacked by the emotion, she decided to script out her interruption, planning exactly what she wanted to say. She thought the conversation went well, but the next day, the woman made a formal complaint against her to HR and questioned the circumstances of her hiring. The complaint indicated she was too sensitive and emotional to be in a leadership position, which is interesting, because the person complaining was a Black woman. The dynamic illustrates that people of color are not always allies to each other. Sometimes, they get caught up in holding each other down, like the proverbial crabs pulling each other back into the pot, rather than working to lift everyone up. People who try to destroy each other come from a perspective of lack and scarcity rather than abundance.

It took months for the two women to work through the issue, and Elsa says using the RIR Protocol to build a bridge has been difficult. In fact, she admits regretting using the RIR Protocol at one point because it felt like it had backfired on her by eliciting the vengeance of the staff member. At one point, she even considered quitting her position. Then, at a leadership conference for superintendents, a speaker said, "Your feelings are hurt. Get over it. Lead." She realized her job was to stay and lead, and that little push gave her what she needed to lean into her own fear and "stuff," and gave her the resolve to stick with it. It was messy, it was hard... and it was worth it.

The RIR Protocol offered her a tool to model that leadership. It does not guarantee that the interaction will be easy or that it will not make it worse; what it does do is allow you to engage with integrity and fidelity to showing up in an authentic and compassionate way that allows you to rise above the noise and be your best self in that moment. It was disappointing that she could not guarantee a happy ending in that interaction, but at least she had a compassionate approach to the messiness instead of one stemming from her own anger or desire for revenge. She saw firsthand that the RIR Protocol is not always pretty, but it allowed her to lean in with this difficult person and continue trying to interrupt and repair.

For a while, even when Elsa acknowledged mistakes and apologized, the woman kept coming after her. Elsa felt like she was under surveillance, and there was no room for her to be a fallible human. Finally, they made some progress when Elsa helped a member of the woman's union, which actually prompted the woman to write and thank her. That gesture felt like a first step toward a better relationship.

Elsa says ultimately, the biggest lesson was the importance of building, maintaining, and staying focused on relationships. Until she found herself struggling with this person, she didn't fully appreciate that relationships—built on interpersonal communication—are the only source of real healing.

UNDERLYING ISSUES

Just because you know the steps doesn't mean a situation will always flow the way you want it to. You can still find yourself flubbing and having uncomfortable interactions. The RIR Protocol does, however, offer the promise of seeing better communication patterns over time, if you consistently use and follow the steps. People will gradually respond better to you, even though you may still have isolated problems.

Bonnie offers a good example of someone not using the RIR Protocol to its full potential. As I shared earlier, she was a principal in a small, Bay Area school district. At the time of this incident, almost a decade ago, she knew the RIR Protocol but wasn't fully living it yet.

Bonnie's incident started at the beginning of a school year. It is commonplace for the principal to make the class lists and then circulate them among the students and teachers. In this case, one teacher came to complain about the list and asked how Bonnie had made the decisions about which students were to be in her class. The teacher said she had too many Latinos, which would make it hard for her to teach. Just by looking at the names, she assumed the kids would not come in prepared to learn at their grade level.

Bonnie says the comment put her back on her heels, and she didn't know how to respond. She recognized that she was appalled and shocked, but she felt caught off guard and didn't know what to do as an administrator. She was the authority figure, but she didn't know how to resolve the issue. She proceeded with what we call a technical interruption, by addressing the class list question and not the comment.

Instead of addressing the underlying problem with the teacher's perspective, she simply justified not changing the class list. She talked about the school's protocol for balancing classes but never directly interrupted the teacher's bias against Latino students (based solely on their names) nor what that would mean for the Latino students in her class.

I think it's important to consider her example, because she'd already learned the RIR Protocol, but she still had work to do. She still wishes she could go back and change this interaction, dealing with the real issue instead of avoiding it. The real issue wasn't the class list but rather the teacher's negative feelings toward and expectations of Brown kids. That conversation needed to happen, but at the time, she didn't know how. Now, in hindsight, she understands how she could interrupt and get to the heart of the matter instead of focusing on surface-level issues, potentially achieving a different outcome. Ad hoc reactions to symptoms don't achieve the same change as working on the underlying problem. Yet, it is important to note that this is not an unusual response even when you know the RIR Protocol. Knowing something is different than being able to do the thing, and if you do not practice normalizing discomfort and practice some rote interruptions that resonate with who you are and how you show up, then it can be difficult to put the RIR Protocol into practice. The key is not to punish yourself when you don't interrupt, but to reflect on why you didn't and continue to work to resolve the issue that got in your way. Remember... you're still making inroads! Sometimes it is as simple as making a promise to yourself that the next time you have the opportunity, you will lean in and interrupt...just that brings a level of consciousness to your decision-making process and increases the likelihood of it happening the next time. Refer to the appendix of resources at the end of this book for tools and motivation to support you along your path.

ADAPTIVE VERSUS TECHNICAL RESPONSES

There are adaptive and technical responses. In a technical response, if something breaks, you fix it. Maybe it broke because of someone else's actions—like a child running around the kitchen and knocking over a glass—but in a technical mindset, you simply repair the broken item rather than addressing the running. By contrast, an adaptive approach takes care of the broken glass while also addressing the root cause that led to that symptom in the first place. In the example above, Bonnie took a technical approach, only talking about the class list instead of what was simmering underneath.

An adaptive approach does not draw on a prescribed right answer, because appropriate responses are fluid depending on the situation, who you're talking to, and what comes up. When I teach people about the RIR Protocol or conduct equity trainings, I use an adaptive approach. I know the material well and have a PowerPoint ready to go, but if people seem stuck and the presentation isn't progressing well, then I name and address that issue.

For instance, I did a presentation for a charter school system with one of the most diverse teaching populations I'd ever seen. We were on the second day of a three-day training series that was six hours each day. When I got to my fourth slide, the tension in the room was palpable. Something was happening in the room that I couldn't put my finger on—a dysfunctional human dynamic—and it was getting in the way of progressing through the material. I kept trying to address it and move on, because we had a lot of work left to do.

There were about seventy people in the room, and no matter what I did, someone would push back and start another discussion that derailed us. Finally, after an hour and a half of trying my best facilitation to get the session moving, I stopped. The director and executive director were in the room, and I said to them, "There's something else happening. Is it okay if I abandon the presentation and we deal with what's happening in the room?" It wasn't just my perception; there was obviously a problem. I applaud their leadership in telling me yes, we could stop.

For the next four hours, I processed what was coming up in the room that wouldn't allow us to move through the content. Had I stayed technical, then I would have simply dragged through the slides at any cost, even if people clearly weren't benefiting from it. As the creator of that content, though, I knew we couldn't move on until we got to the heart of what people were feeling. So, I dusted off my best counseling skills. We had a listening circle, and it ended up being the most powerful of the three sessions. The next day flew by because we'd overcome the earlier barriers through direct engagement.

When you first learn the RIR Protocol, you're in the technical space of following the steps in order and learning what they mean. Once you truly feel it and know it, though, you reach a place of seeking to understand in all your interactions. Then, your responses become adaptive. You intuitively understand when to interrupt with "I'm not sure what you mean—tell me more," and when you need a stronger reaction, like "Wow, that's super offensive. Why would you say that to me?" Both come from a place of truth, and their appropriateness depends on context.

Too often in difficult conversations, we can find ourselves swayed by someone saying we're "coming at them" or being too harsh, when really, they're detouring to avoid talking about the issue. We're simply being direct with them about whatever the issue is. Unfortunately, directness is not something that has been rewarded in our society, thus we end up sidetracking the actual issue and rarely reaching any resolution. The RIR Protocol allows us to remain grounded in reality and our values, which then facilitates a constructive response. Being direct about what's really happening doesn't make you the bad guy.

Some people like to bait us over and over until we react—and then cast us as the bad guy for reacting. So sometimes the interruption has to be strong, in the context of the big picture regarding a person's pattern of behavior toward us. The important part is that however we decide to interrupt, it needs to come from a place of controlling our emotions and not letting our emotions control us. If my interruption is strong, it's because I've chosen it to be strong—not because I'm afraid.

An adaptive stance means staying open to the broader context and considering all the factors at play, not simply employing a formula. It also leaves room for us to be surprised—to have an "aha" moment. By contrast, a technical stance risks simply focusing on eliminating our discomfort or solving the issue without getting to the heart of it, which means we never resolve the underlying cause. As a result, it can happen again. If you treat your diabetes simply with meds, you still have diabetes; but if you get healthy, possibly lose weight (if that is your issue), exercise, and eat less sugar, you may be able to modify or eliminate the treatment.[4]

It's natural to start the RIR Protocol in a more technical place, but the goal should be to become adaptive over time. The more you practice, the more inspired and flexible you can be.

THE COLOR LINE

When I had to adapt the charter school training that just wasn't working, the majority of the people in the room were people of color, which rarely happens. Still, the people of color were not the people in power. They were the teachers and aides. So even though about 70 percent of attendees were people of color, the White 30 percent were mostly in executive and leadership positions.

This particular session was on culturally relevant pedagogy, and we'd talked about understanding critical race theory as a lens the previous day. The first day went well because it was a validation for people of color and provided "aha" moments for White folks who didn't already know the

---

4   Please note that I understand that diabetes is more complex than this and that there can be many factors at play with this medical condition. In this example, I am speaking more to my family's issues and history and attempting to make a larger point about symptoms versus root causes.

material. When we got down to being culturally relevant and proficient, though, people felt the material was all talk. It didn't reflect how they saw the organization's approach or intent in real life.

People of color in the room felt hurt and needed to share their stories of being marginalized in the system they worked in. This particular system is known for being very progressive. If you're in one of the most progressive systems in the state and still feel invisible and marginalized as a person of color, then there's a disconnect somewhere. The White-centered leadership had one vision of itself, while the actual experience of employees of color within the organization was very different.

The more academic, historical content on the first day seemed denser and more difficult, which made me think the second day would be a breeze. In practice, though, the real-life applications stirred up unresolved, personal hurt we needed to address if we were ever going to move forward in a productive way. The second day brought the theory home and asked people to self-reflect, which exposed a number of barriers.

I appreciate the leadership for being willing to hear the feedback and adjust course. That outcome was the RIR Protocol in action. The White leaders were the minority in the room, but they were open to listening.

One activity I used that day was a color line, a powerful technique developed by The National SEED Project.[5] In it, people answer a variety of questions, including the following:

- I can, if I wish, arrange to be in the company of people of my race most of the time.
- When I am told about our national heritage or about "civilization," I am shown that people of my color made it what it is.
- If I should need to move, I can be pretty sure of renting or purchasing housing in an area which I can afford and in which I want to live.
- If I need to move, I can be pretty sure that my neighbors in such a location will be neutral or pleasant to me.
- I can be sure that my children will be given curricular materials that testify to the existence of their race.
- I can swear, or dress in secondhand clothes, or not answer letters, without having people attribute those choices to the bad morals, the poverty, or the illiteracy of my race.
- I am never asked to speak for all the people of my racial group.
- If a traffic cop pulls me over or if the IRS audits my tax

---

5   Peggy McIntosh, "'White Privilege: Unpacking the Invisible Knapsack' and 'Some Notes for Facilitators,'" SEED: The National SEED Project, https://nationalseedproject.org/Key-SEED-Texts/White-privilege-unpacking-the-invisible-knapsack.

return, I can be sure I haven't been singled out because of my race.

- I can go shopping alone most of the time, pretty well assured that I will not be followed or harassed.
- And so on.

Based on their responses to the questions, they receive a score from zero to 125. Once the scores are calculated, participants line up in the room according to their numbers, creating a powerful visual representation of the color line. It's called the color line because almost without exception, the darkest people in the room will be closest to zero, and the White people will cluster in the 100 to 125 range. The 100s tend to be women, because even though they have White privilege, they still face gender discrimination. White men tend to rank closest to the top. The activity sheds light on the experiences of different identities and gives you a visual demonstration of how privilege operates, which is quite powerful.

The exercise comes from the popular article "White Privilege: Unpacking the Invisible Knapsack" by Peggy McIntosh. She was a college professor initially interested in women's studies. In trying to prove there was a glass ceiling for women, she realized race actually trumped gender. She even calls herself out as a well-meaning White person who didn't know how to take constructive feedback from people of color. She finally caught herself and sharing her journey has been a powerful tool.

Using the color line helped this group heal through more perspective and understanding. There are ten feet between each number. I'm a twelve on the color line and typically the darkest person in the room. The next person might be thirty feet away, and 75 percent of the room is White and at the 120 mark. Between myself and that mark, the color of the participants gradually gets lighter, going from Black, to mixed, to Latinx, to Asians. Of course, there are some exceptions that make me ask questions. If I see a White woman at eighty, I wonder who she's married to and who her grandkids are; almost 100 percent of the time, she's in an interracial relationship or has grandchildren of color and now understands what White privilege means through that experience.

What was powerful about the exercise in this particular workshop was that all the people of color were between one and thirty on the line, and then the White people were far away, with some all the way at 125. It provided such a stark visual.

When I conduct the exercise, I usually walk the line and talk about desegregation of schools and what it was like for Black kids being bused to White schools during Brown v. Board of Education. As I do the walk, people's faces show their reactions. They actually become the roles I mention. Some White people won't make eye contact with me—even though they're adults and not complicit in the original offense I am describing. A Black man once said "Sellout," when I talked about going to White schools. In his mind, doing so meant abandoning the Black community.

When I used the exercise in this case, because I took an adaptive approach, I modified it. I thought about how it's always a Black person doing the long, arduous walk. There have been times I've wanted to cry while walking and talking about desegregation, because it stirs up so much emotion for me. This time, I asked the White end of the line who wanted to walk with me. I got a White person to change the dynamic: instead of talking about using Black bodies to desegregate White schools, I asked what would have happened if White kids had also gone to Black schools. The situation would have been very different if, instead of taking all the Black kids out of their communities and putting them in White communities where they weren't wanted, we'd actually brought White kids into Black communities and started to build community together.

A White woman volunteer walked with me as I did this thought experiment, and as she walked by, everyone in the lower numbers high-fived her. It gave me chills. She was visibly nervous, and everyone said how brave she was, which speaks to how people of color have been conditioned to care for how White people feel. It also shows how White kids coming into a Black neighborhood could be welcomed. People wouldn't want them to feel threatened.

No one cared how I felt when I did the walk, but her experience was different. In a way, it's beautiful that people of color care about how White people feel coming into our spaces. It also points out the lack of reciprocity. How can we all care about and support each other, conveying empathy and a sense of community to people of color? How can White people begin to take responsibility for helping people of color feel comfortable in predominantly White spaces, as people of color do for White people in their spaces all the time?

I'd done the color line activity many times, but never in that way. For that particular audience, the adaptation proved transformative. The RIR Protocol calls for giving what we need. In that instance, we needed something different because the team was struggling.

HEALING THE YOUNGER SELF

Poppy is a CEO in the UK mental health sector. I met her in late 2020 through a mutual friend, who said she was doing great consulting work for his company, and he knew immediately the two of us had to meet.

We spoke by phone for the first time without an agenda, and talking to her felt like a homecoming. I felt I'd known her my whole life. She's very down to earth, brilliant, funny, and honest. We had a lovely conversation.

She said the gods were on her side because she was going through some trauma and had decided she needed to talk to someone who was not directly related to the issue. She felt our introduction came at a fortuitous time. I said I'd be happy to do a free coaching session to walk her through using the RIR Protocol to address the interpersonal problem she was experiencing. The impact of the work was so powerful for her that she invited me to come back and speak to thirty-five CEOs in the mental health sector.

She's Bangladeshi, and most of her colleagues are White, cisgender men. She's one of the only women of color at her level in her field. She asked to join a particular professional network, and one of her colleagues from another organization turned her down, citing a technicality about the type of organization she worked for. She thought her contributions could be valuable and they might be able to make an exception, but the policy seemed clear cut, so she took the response at face value.

A couple years later, she was getting ready to leave the position, and a White man was slated to take over her role. She suggested that he reach out to her colleague and try to join the network, because she still thought it would be valuable. He told her he'd already been invited, even though he'd only had the role for a few weeks.

This experience sent her over the edge. Questions began

swirling in her mind. Had she been turned down because of her race, because people didn't like her, or why? She's interested in the mental health field because she has her own mental health challenges, and after this incident, she found herself in a spiral.

As we talked, I asked her what she recognized. She said the feelings brought up her seven-year-old self, who never seemed to be good enough for others. She said she felt like a child again, serving tea to her family. In her traditional Bangladeshi family, girls were not supposed to be seen or heard—they were there to serve. Her male family members would gather, and her job was to serve them, but she wasn't allowed to stay and participate in the conversation. In her professional role, she felt triggered by the situation of being in the room but not having her voice valued. She could serve through her job, but she couldn't stay and engage as an equal with other leaders.

She felt fear, anger, and frustration at not being invited to the network and not receiving recognition for the perspective and experience she brought to the table. She felt like she was in a position of weakness in which others determined her future for her because she was a woman and Brown. She raised the notion of historical trauma, having grown up in a family without a right to her own voice.

In fact, everything about her career is at odds with her

family's expectations. She also feared the consequences of speaking out. She felt angry but also afraid of people stereotyping her as an angry woman of color and questioning her credibility. She didn't have an option to interrupt her successor, because he wasn't actually the person who had snubbed her—he's simply how she found out she'd been snubbed.

She also recognized she was in self-preservation mode. She felt herself shutting down, because she feared if she got too involved, her mental health would suffer—and, in fact, it did.

She was angry at the gentleman who'd denied her entry into the program. He was one of the CEOs and supposedly a friend. There were interpersonal aspects, but the experience also stirred up a tremendous number of unresolved feelings from her past. The RIR Protocol operates on multiple levels. In order to have an interpersonal interaction, you still have to do intrapersonal work. To show up fully with another person, you need to identify your interests and what's happening for you inside.

When she first got denied, she was told it was for a technical reason—the committee wasn't for people in her role. She didn't push, even though she figured they could make an exception. As it turned out, they could—but for whom? Apparently, a White man, but not her.

After she recognized what the interaction triggered in her—all the childhood trauma, fear, anger, frustration, and need for self-preservation—her interruption was to talk to someone about it. She felt like she was spiraling out of control. She started abusing substances, and she needed help. Her first step toward interrupting was talking to me. We didn't know each other, but she felt I completely understood her and made her feel safe. She took the risk of having the conversation and found a positive result. Initially, I planned to help her interrupt on the interpersonal level, by speaking with her colleague. I talked about addressing systems that perpetuate discrimination.

Through our conversation, though, she ended up asking herself how she could write her own story without blame or shame. How could she remove the little girl from the dialogue? Through self-reflection, she recognized that the little girl was hurt and reacting, because she took the exclusion personally. She felt the colleague wanted her successor but not her. She interrupted herself by removing the inner child's reaction and examining how to show up as a CEO and woman of color to interrupt interpersonally from a more empowered place.

In other words, her response was two-fold. First, she had to interrupt her own historical trauma so she could have a conversation as an adult, rather than a seven-year-old who wanted to lash out in anger. Then, as an adult professional, she could say, "This isn't about blame or shame. I want you to understand the impact." She told her story and enumerated the talent, insight, and opportunities the network lost by excluding her. She's good at what she does, and others missed out on the chance to collaborate with her. As a result, she framed the conversation from a place of power.

Through our conversation, she didn't devalue, dismiss, or diminish the little girl; instead, she healed her so she could move forward. We all have past experiences to grapple with. In my case, I adopted lying as a defense mechanism in childhood, and in adulthood, I had to self-interrupt because the behavior no longer served me. It was a bad habit I had to break through healing myself, not fighting against myself. By bringing those childhood issues out into the open, we can take responsibility and find our power in the present. Poppy's experiences made her who she is today: an accomplished woman who speaks up because she never wants to be subservient again. When the little girl creeps back in, she can remember she's not a child anymore—she has power and control over herself.

Her intrapersonal interruption was to reconcile with the little girl, and her interpersonal one was to share her experience with the other CEOs. Her repair focused on self-care and healing on a personal level. She stopped drinking and started taking yoga. She went back to therapy. Once she had more emotional resources, we talked about how to address the systemic discrimination, and she decided to make a leadership commitment. As a woman of color, she recognized she had to stay strong and continue to pave the way for other women like her, without regressing or hiding. She shared her four commitments with the CEOs, and four other people raised their hands and said they wanted to commit, too.

She helped form a committee to talk about equity and how to apply the commitments. All the CEOs are from different mental health organizations, so together, they can make a large impact. The other CEOs who joined her wrote their own personal statements incorporating the four principles, and a few weeks later, three more joined in.

She sees momentum. They've started a blog and opened a dialogue about repair within each organization. Some CEOs want to do the work personally but don't see an opening within their organizations currently, so those barriers are part of the discussion. Poppy emphasizes that the important part is taking a step toward growth, not achieving perfection.

After Poppy's interruption with the network, she felt they had made great progress. However, it was short-lived, and she got another opportunity to interrupt when the network announced it was putting on a public panel discussion. Members of the royal family would attend, and it would be a big event. Six days before, she had not received an invitation, and her inner child got triggered again. The panel had four White men, and again, she wrestled with feelings of exclusion and devaluation. When she called to talk to the organizers, they made excuses about politics. She recognized she was angry and knew she needed to demand a change. Even though she was angry, I consider her approach Compassionate Dialogue™. Compassion doesn't mean every interaction will be easy; rather, it stems from the commitment to connect and create change. By the time the panel took place, two women had joined the lineup, and she was one of them. It also proved that when pressed, people can move mountains if they wish so there is no reason to settle...at least not without a fight.

She told me that because she'd spelled out her commitments to herself and her values, she swallowed her pride and attended. I suggested she reframe her response—she didn't swallow her pride but rather took them to task for failing to organize a high-profile event with intentionality. She was a badass. She effected change, demanded equity, and then took her rightful place speaking in front of the royal family. She nailed it. She'd only recently learned the RIR Protocol but managed to shift a dynamic that has been stagnant in the UK for decades. She stood up for what was right and beat systemic racism in that instance—so she can put the little girl to rest.

Through her personal work, she impacted the intrapersonal, the interpersonal, and the systemic. Not every use of the RIR Protocol hits all three levels, but her experience did.

RESOLUTION DOESN'T ALWAYS EQUAL FORGIVENESS

Bob Smith is a White male in his sixties who works as a district attorney and leads a Youth and Family Services program in Northern California. He's committed to supporting youth who are in danger of going off the path. I met him a few years ago when I worked for a mentoring program. I was recruiting and training people to do group mentorship, since we had such a large, longstanding waiting list for one-on-one mentors. He was part of the training, and I thought he was a good guy who really loved kids. He wanted to make a difference and has spent his whole life trying to figure out how to make an impact.

We became friends, and I asked if he would let me interview him for the Conversation Starter Cards™. His interview was phenomenal and a moving experience for both of us. During the interview, I pushed back on some of what he said, and he was willing to learn and grow. He hadn't had many experiences of people forcing him to look at himself and what he was saying. He mostly socialized with affluent White people, even though he works with young, diverse populations facing difficulties. He said he was "an old White guy" who "didn't know what he didn't know yet." We started a friendship.

A couple of years later, he asked if we could go for coffee to discuss a personal issue. He said he had a longtime friend who, at his suggestion, met a new partner on eHarmony after losing his wife. They were having dinner together, and Bob started telling a story about being invited to a dinner of high-powered women to tell them what men look for in a dating ad. Apparently, he'd said, "I hate to say it, but the majority of men are just looking for a wet mucous lining." He meant it as a way of commiserating with the women, acknowledging that men are dogs, and in that initial group presentation, the women laughed. His point was that there's no use in agonizing over what to write, when most men aren't even reading it.

In retelling the story in front of his friend's new partner, though, he apparently triggered her and stirred up all kinds of old trauma for her. She didn't understand the context and never wanted to spend time with Bob and his wife again. He felt terrible, because he didn't want to upset her and felt she had missed the point of the story. It did not matter, however, as she pretty much decided she did not ever want to spend time with him again. Can we say, "ghosting?"

After some cajoling from her new partner, she ended up agreeing to allow me to mediate a conversation between

Bob and herself. Initially, I began with encouraging him to take an intrapersonal journey, because he didn't see anything wrong with the story. He understood the difference between intent and impact, which is why he wanted to use the RIR Protocol, but he saw himself as "not that guy." Her reaction, though, made him wonder if he *was* "that guy."

He felt guilt and shame. He's typically perceived as vivacious, witty, and quick, so he felt he'd grossly misjudged his audience. He wasn't used to worrying about who might misunderstand his intentions. As we talked, he wasn't trying to excuse his behavior; he genuinely wanted to repair the situation. However, he felt a dissonance because he didn't feel he'd done anything wrong in retelling a story—in fact, the women in the initial interaction had invited him because of his candor. He'd retold the story with the intent of illustrating how lucky he and his friend were no longer to be on the dating market, but the impact was something else entirely.

As a result, he began to think about other interactions and wonder whether he'd gone too far. He assumes good intentions and that people know him, but this woman's reaction made him recognize that his internal view of himself might not match the impression he makes on others. He began to see how people could misperceive what he says.

His interruption was to ask himself how his behaviors and

statements could get misconstrued. He didn't want to have another negative interaction like the one with his friend's partner, so he began thinking about what he might need to change in himself and the steps he could take to exercise more caution toward others' feelings. As he put it, "When you're writing a new script with new people, you have to be more conscious." Previously, he'd assumed he was who he was, and everyone should give him the benefit of the doubt. However, he learned in behaving that way, he could harm other people and relationships he cared about, like the one with his friend.

When I mediated the interpersonal conversation, it went okay. She was open to listening and talking, even though I was a stranger who obviously felt invested in Bob and his family but didn't know her. At the same time, she'd already made up her mind and was not going to change it. She was in her own story and triggers. I asked her point-blank whether she wanted to heal the situation, and she said she didn't think so, which was good to know. That way, Bob could focus on the divorce rather than trying to connect with her. It was her prerogative not to engage with him further, especially since she didn't have a history with him.

Because she was not interested in remaining in the relationship, his repair stemmed from himself: he chose to be more cognizant of who he's interacting with and how his behavior can impact his relationships. If he has a history with someone, there's more flexibility—but when he doesn't, then he needs to be more cautious. Hopefully, the woman will also reflect on her own feelings of being stuck. Bob still socializes with his friend, but he doesn't engage with the partner, which limits the friendship. They used to spend a few nights a week together, but now they only ride bikes once a week.

Bob's story illustrates that when we talk about repair, it's not always a happy ending. Repair is just resolution.

SPEAKING UP

Rochelle, who'd been accused of showing preference to Black children, approached the conversation with her director from a place of compassion and self-care, not shaming or blaming. Still, she felt scared, which was natural and not a feeling the RIR Protocol could make disappear. She wanted to hold her director accountable, but with the intention of making the situation right.

Rochelle was understandably hurt by the director's initial comment. It had an embedded accusation against her character. Her interruption focused on the double standard. She gave the example of the district adopting McGraw-Hill: the White staff members, leaders, and organizations choosing those textbooks never asked whether there might be a White agenda. The Chief Academic Officer at that time was White, but no one said they chose the textbook because of race. That example provided a counter scenario to give context on the accusation against her.

It went much better than she expected. She'd anticipated White tears and White fragility, but she got an amazing conversation. She felt that the relationship improved. Her experience shows what can happen if both parties are willing to deepen the relationship through compassion. She said the only time we need to be racializing anything is when we're talking about who is impacted and how, but people shouldn't racialize her motivation. If someone insists on racializing her motivation, then they have to do it for the White people in leadership roles, too. This director heard what she was saying and expressed appreciation for the feedback. They began to approach the issue differently, with deeper candor.

So even though using the RIR Protocol was scary for her, it was also extremely successful. It was the right approach, and she felt good in the end. She felt she'd spoken her truth and been heard. She achieved the best result possible, because the other person heard her, responded, and participated in the repair by removing that racial lens and focusing on the population the program impacted.

To effect real change, you have to learn to communicate to be understood, not to be right. Understanding comes from focusing on the relationship and seeing the individual value in the other person. When we value them, we're also valuing ourselves—that's empathy. We're all having a human experience, doing the best that we can with what we've got in the moment. Your best or my best right now may not be great, but it's what we've got. If we can bring that understanding to the relationship, we can support each other in growing.

PAUSE AND PRACTICE

- Are there relationships you can think of that you have some unresolved issue with?

- How much time do you spend thinking about the person or the issue?

- What gets in the way of you addressing the issue with the person?

CHAPTER 6

HOW DO WE USE COMPASSIONATE DIALOGUE™ IN AN ORGANIZATION OR SYSTEM?

Nicole is a director of curriculum and instruction. Her district worked with Epoch for a year, training all their leadership, from site principals to central office administrators. We structured the training as a project-based cycle of inquiry, where they got to choose among eight topics for the year.

For example, one was disproportionality with children of

color in special education. I facilitated the topic of implicit bias. I ended up with about fifteen admins in my group, and Nicole was one of them. We did a one-day training on what implicit bias is, and then we went into the RASCI Model[6], which looks at action planning through the lens of equity.

Every principal and director chose a project they wanted to work on regarding this topic over the course of the year. The requirement was that the project had to be grounded in a real problem of practice and executable during the year. Then, I coached them on strategies during our quarterly face-to-face gatherings. Nicole's project dealt with adopting new textbooks to meet the state's revised social studies standards.

She wanted to create a rubric that would help the district make a decision and keep equity front and center as they reviewed various textbooks for adoption. Her guiding question was: if using an equity lens isn't natural for decisionmakers, then how might the rubric keep those concerns at the forefront? Using the principles of critical race theory that we'd talked about, along with other implicit bias material, she created a rubric that asked specific questions about the textbooks. For example, were people of color literally in the book's margins? If you think about your high school

---

6   RASCI stands for Responsible, Accountable, Supportive, Consulted, and Informed. The model helps identify a participant's responsibilities and role within a project. Read more at: https://www.goodcore.co.uk/blog/a-guide-to-the-raci-rasci-model/.

history textbook, you can probably remember the stories in colored boxes off to the side. The chapter would tell an overarching story and then have occasional sidebars—were those the only places students would see people of color?

Once Nicole wrote the rubric, she rolled it out with her team. I still remember her texting me to say, "I just shared the rubric with my team, and it's crickets in here, and I'm freaking out." I told her to take a deep breath and use the RIR Protocol. If they don't like it, use the Protocol. If they love it, use the Protocol. Since the rubric approach was new to them, though, she first needed to give them a minute to let everything sink in and see what feelings came up for them.

THE RIR PROTOCOL IN AN ORGANIZATIONAL SETTING

When we think about the organizational application of the RIR Protocol, we still use the same principles of recognize, interrupt, repair. The recognition, though, relates to what your feelings are regarding policies and procedures in the organization that are potentially problematic, and also gets you thinking about the impact it is having—intended and unintended. For example, let's look at legacy preferencing in institutions. If you see that form of nepotism, what feelings arise for you about that process? Who is it benefiting and who is being left out? How do people get hired in systems, and do feelings arise for you regarding how equitable those processes are? The goal is to recognize your feelings around the way the organization functions and look for the problematic practices that keep systems of inequity in place.

At a government level, you could consider the feelings that arise for you around racial profiling; as well as the impact that practice has on the particular targets of the behavior. When I consider Latinxs being stopped at the border because agents assume they're not US citizens, feelings arise for me. It's a systemic problem, not an interpersonal one. If I'm feeling angry about racial profiling, then I need to look at ways to interrupt the inequitable practice or system. The steps are exactly the same, but the scale is different—I'm looking at a policy, procedure, or practice. When an issue is relational, I devise a way to interrupt the person who said or did something that triggered me. When it's personal, I figure out how to interrupt myself.

The recognition step of the RIR Protocol signals when something's amiss. You and I can go our whole day and never be triggered by anything. But if something triggers us, our body and intuition are telling us something is wrong. The first R is essential, because it brings the problem to the forefront of our consciousness. If I go my whole day, nothing triggers me, and I don't recognize anything, bad situations may still have happened; however, they didn't impact me and trigger my first R.

Many organizations have taken being politically correct to heart. They go to great lengths to use inclusive language and practice equity, which stems from the worthy intention of dismantling oppression. The problem, though, is that being PC doesn't help in the long run if it means you can't get to root causes and talk about the truth. There's a difference between being PC and being compassionate. I can be compassionate and still be very direct. Political correctness is usually more about omission. We contort ourselves to avoid saying what we really mean and instead focus on avoiding feeling or causing discomfort. PC culture puts limits on what we can talk about in polite company, which means we don't ever talk about what we need to talk about.

NOT INDIVIDUALS, SYSTEMS

Like many people around him, Dr. Martin Luther King, Jr. recognized inequities. What set him apart was actually taking steps toward acting on his beliefs. He effected change through his work as a pastor, being in the right place at the right time, and knowing the right people. He had leverage as a leader, but he couldn't do the work by himself. I believe lessons during Black History Month often do damage by making him the savior without acknowledging the foundation that others laid before him and all the supports that lifted him up to do what he had to do. There were myriad moving parts.

The same goes for Rosa Parks. She was the icon, but she did not do the work alone. We so often teach Black history as a story of rugged individualism, but that stance in essence disempowers the whole culture. It's important to understand that Rosa Parks, the NAACP, and all the folks in the civil rights movement planned months and months in advance for her to not give up her seat that day. They collaborated on a conscious act, which is empowering. If she's just an individual who randomly felt tired one day and decided not to move, though, then you're relying on luck rather than organizing. But when you dig deeper, you understand why this narrative is important in keeping the status quo of ethnic marginalization. To teach history this way actually disempowers the movement and the brilliance of the people in it. It maintains white supremacy by holding up supposedly exceptional people and diminishing everyone else in the process and failing to acknowledge the brilliance of the movement that changed the face of this country.

Imagine teaching the truth, that oppressed people organized and created an outcome leading to the Civil Rights Act. There were so many people combining their planning and brainpower to reach that achievement. As Chinua Achebe says, "Until the lions have their own historians, the history of the hunt will always glorify the hunter."

At an organizational level, the RIR Protocol involves getting others to practice it, too, whether you explicitly name the Protocol to them or not. Organizational Compassionate Dialogue™ is the hardest, but it also makes the greatest impact. It's the next evolution of all the work you do on yourself and with others. In order to get the systemic, organizational change, you have to harness interpersonal engagement, because individuals make up organizations. Recognizing and interrupting problems within an organization requires many smaller interruptions and repairs to get people on board with the need for change. The work happens at all levels. You do your own work, work with your peers, and build a coalition to work together on the system.

As we near the close of this book, I hope you find yourself inspired to pursue more of your own learning and consider taking another look at our history—the story of Rosa Parks, for example, and more—through a more critical lens.

EQUITY AUDITS[7]

Equity audits are tremendous opportunities to really take a look at yourself and your space. What message are you sending, even indirectly? You can tell a lot about a person and an organization by what they cultivate in their environment. Within one minute of being in a space, I can see the priorities reflected back at me. And if I can—that means so can students and so can clients. One quick question we look

---

7   For more information and resources on Equity Audits, refer to the Appendix.

at to start this process is: what pictures are on the walls, on your websites, and do they offer diverse representation?

We approach equity audits as a partner exercise: one person gives feedback on another's space, and they switch. At first, these conversations can be difficult because feedback can be hard to hear. However, an underlying point of this exercise is to normalize that conversations about areas of growth are normal and necessary for us as we continue to hone our practice. We recommend equity audits at least three times a year, and they typically become easier over time. By the third audit, most people are on the same page: "We're in this together. I'm trying to make your space and mine more culturally relevant and better for the students and clients we serve."

Equity audits can go beyond physical spaces, too. Some tools for businesses consider websites, for instance. Which stock images does the site use, and what language does it use? One organization we worked with served people dealing with difficult transitions in their lives. The website used diverse stock photos, but the photos didn't relate to the clients at all. Everyone in the pictures wore a suit. The images portrayed a particular vision of the middle class, which didn't connect to the people the organization served. More appropriate, inclusive images might have included hoodies and tattoos. Equity includes reflecting the people served, not just putting up any Black or Brown face.

COMPASSIONATE DIALOGUE™ AT THE DISTRICT LEVEL

When I met Julie, she was the superintendent of a school district as well as a White, out-lesbian woman who was a vocal, passionate advocate for equity. She first learned about Epoch through our Conversation Starter Cards™, which she originally stumbled on by accident and ended up buying for the entire leadership team. Because of her large purchase, I offered to give a training, so they'd understand the RIR Protocol and feel comfortable using it.

When Julie learned the RIR Protocol, she realized it was exactly what she'd been looking for. She wanted a scalable process to engage people throughout the organization. Instead of training on a specific topic like implicit bias, microaggressions, or culturally relevant pedagogy, she saw the RIR Protocol as an overarching framework everyone could use to talk about anything.

She decided the entire district would use Compassionate Dialogue™ as a tool to communicate with each other. She realized for change to occur, she needed to look beyond administrators alone and also include the school board in using the RIR Protocol. Principals began using the Protocol in their schools, too. She thought if everyone in the district spoke the same language, they could improve their ability to act on important issues, such as inclusion.

At every school board meeting, they started by pulling a card or watching and practicing based on one of our YouTube videos, because she considered using the RIR to be a critical skill. She focused on language evolution. In introducing the RIR Protocol, she presented examples of marginalizing language within the organization that wasn't intended to be harmful but was still problematic. She knew the more you practice, the more you get comfortable with it—and the less challenging it becomes.

She's since moved to a new district in Southern California and brought the RIR Protocol there because she had such great results previously. She knew it worked. She'd even started including a slide on Epoch and the RIR Protocol in every presentation she did, because she believed if everyone used it, organizations and larger society would begin to see positive changes. At her new district, she has started with her board, which helped shape conversation around a new framework for fair and accessible education for everyone (The FAIR Act). The district wanted representative curriculum that was inclusive to the LGBTQ+ community, but the district has a large conservative-leaning parent base who were concerned about this particular topic. In short, they were okay with all the other parts of the act except the "gay part."

With Julie being an openly gay White woman, they began to make inaccurate connections. For example, people misconstrued the initiative as wanting to teach their kids to be gay. Julie said the RIR Protocol was absolutely crucial in facilitating these conversations and helping her administrators, who were getting the brunt of the criticism from families and community organizations. By once again rolling out the RIR Protocol for every staff member and student, she was working toward the big-picture possibilities.

The district was in the process of scaling the use of the RIR Protocol when COVID hit. She wanted to figure out ways to keep the conversation going and avoid losing momentum. Based on the experience in her other district, she knows the value of having a strong, district-wide foundation in compassionate communication. She uses the RIR Protocol to hold people accountable for what they say and do, which is the Protocol's power at the systemic level. It holds us accountable to our mission statement, vision, policies, and procedures. If they're not in alignment with who we say we are, how do we get them into alignment through the RIR Protocol?

Julie's experience using the RIR Protocol also dovetails with her experience as a lesbian in challenging stereotypes about gay people—for instance, that she would want to hit on every woman in the world just because she's gay. A big component of this work is challenging stereotypes like this one that marginalize groups and make it easy for people to discriminate.

In Julie's case, she knew it felt easier to "blame" her than it would be for those making those comments to confront their own homophobia. But she didn't let that stop her. She's always spoken truth to power to a degree, but the RIR Protocol gave her a tool allowing her to engage more skillfully in difficult conversations. She began using it at the organizational level but says she's also found that it's a way for her to check herself around her own biases. She's always evolving through the process.

Using the RIR Protocol has changed the way she approaches interactions. Before learning it, she was more defensive about difficult subjects. Now, she has a tool for choosing how to interact. It grounds her so she can show up and take care of business instead of getting lost in her emotions and reactions. She says she feels more empowered as a result—in who she is and in the work she does—which helps overcome some of her personal doubts around having grown up gay in the Catholic church and being a high-profile figure. She can face feelings of danger with a sense of focus and purpose.

The RIR Protocol is easier for people like me and Julie: we are already direct. This work is harder for people who are more timid and who communicate more passively (refer to the Communication Styles handout and the 4 Affects handout in the Appendix or the discussion of the same in Chapter 2). We all, however, can benefit; for me and Julie, the RIR Protocol softens our edges and helps us channel our directness with compassion. For those who are in the opposite boat, the RIR Protocol builds confidence and encourages them to speak up in situations in which they would have otherwise felt guilt or shame about holding back.

Julie's story, in particular, is powerful because it provides an example of educating a system to use an equity lens for evaluating practices, policies, and procedures—and then to change them. On the intrapersonal level, the focus is on monitoring myself. At an organizational level, I have to monitor myself *and* create a baseline that allows everyone to engage. I can still interrupt and use the RIR Protocol on a system; it's more complex—but it is worth it!

ORGANIZATIONAL CHANGE TO PERSONAL CHANGE

Anyone of any race or gender can raise the flag and interrupt. It's an injustice in itself if only people of color start a dialogue. The RIR Protocol can also flow in any direction. Generally, the trajectory goes from intrapersonal to interpersonal to organizational, but Julie came at it from a different direction. Once she'd seen transformation in her organization, she started using it on a personal level. The RIR Protocol gave her a compassionate way to deal with her Catholic father, who had a problem with her being an out lesbian. She'd always had to stand up for herself, but the compassionate RIR piece gave her a way to do so without taking on all his bias, judgment, anger, and other emotions.

Her example shows that you can start wherever it feels right and grow from there. The systemic application tends to come into play when someone surfaces a problem. The organization needs to address a policy or procedural issue, and the RIR Protocol offers a way to do so. We must remember, though, that we can't completely address an issue at the organizational or systemic level until we've addressed the individuals who have contributed to the system (i.e., the gatekeepers).

You can enter the process anywhere, and then it will flow from there. You can enter on the interpersonal level and then work on yourself and your organization. You can start with your organization and flow down to yourself. You can start with yourself and flow up. The RIR Protocol becomes an innate process of your communication. It's now my lens on everything I do.

Julie was able to get buy-in because she was fully invested in and embodying Compassionate Dialogue™. It was non-negotiable. She also had an upbringing that got her used to adversity, so she had her own strategies to bring to the table. When you feel marginalized, you figure out ways to negotiate that situation. Your personal experience can and should help inform your organizational work, and vice versa.

REPAIRING BEHAVIORS, NOT PEOPLE

When Julie became the superintendent and began focusing on equity, Jordi had just finished his dissertation work on alternative education programs in the district. He approached her and said he wanted to be a part of whatever she was doing. He jokes that telling a superintendent you want to be a part of their initiative means doing the work, but he was happy to, because equity is his passion.

His dissertation was about getting at the root cause of students ending up in alt ed. He wanted to understand how students get expelled and sent to alternative education settings. Through his research, he built relationships in the district office, even though he wasn't an employee at that point. Because he was a relative outsider, he had an entrée into discussions and environments he couldn't have accessed as a district admin. Through his particular perspective interviewing kids and staff, he developed trust and uncovered many of the issues around race that represented the root causes of the alt ed situation. He saw that a shift needed to happen.

He volunteered to be a part of the equity work. When he met with Julie, she showed him the Conversation Starter Cards™, and he said, "Oh, my God, these are spicy." He'd seen the scenarios in the cards happen all the time in the district. As a result, he wanted to learn the RIR Protocol. The two of them began practicing together with the cards.

Every single staff meeting would start off with a card. He quickly recognized the impact the practice was having on his admin team.

For example, because people knew they'd be practicing the RIR Protocol, they started bringing their own scenarios to the meetings and asking whether they'd chosen an acceptable interruption or if there might be a better way. The admins had rich, deep conversations by using the RIR Protocol. Whereas some people had initially been hesitant or unsure why he was using the cards, once they could apply the RIR to their own interactions, they saw its value. He, in turn, saw the practice beginning to change the system. Interruptions became easier for everyone because they'd been practicing. The scenarios on the cards connected to the issues at their sites, and vice versa.

Gradually, the whole RIR Protocol became more natural and ingrained in the system. Each piece grew easier with practice because people began developing a repertoire of strategies. Initially, they struggled with wanting to repair or change the offending person. Finally, though, he got them to understand that the repair was about the issue or the information. He said the goal was not to win the "Woke Olympics." Rather, the repair needed to address the information or issue that led them to interrupt.

He says once they had that understanding, everything

shifted. The RIR Protocol became real for them. They weren't trying to change people but rather repair what had been said or done. In their case, the problems arose from how they were doing business. The compassionate approach led to shifts in disciplining kids and staff, away from punishment and toward repairing the issue.

Admins tend to be fixers and doers. Changing the lens away from fixing the person and toward fixing the issue led to change in the system. Jordi says all the administrative, certificated, and classified staff practice the RIR Protocol now. The impact is tangible. In a recent webinar, someone said something offensive, and a secretary, who is a classified staff, and considered by some as are relatively low-level staff position, used the RIR Protocol to interrupt and repair in the moment with one of the admins. That was a powerful shift and one that would not have happened prior to the introduction of the RIR Protocol.

The RIR Protocol serves as an equalizer, and this secretary felt empowered to engage and interrupt the comment. She then repaired the information, not the person. Jordi called her after the meeting to praise her. She didn't violate a norm or embarrass anyone, but she addressed the issue. Her interruption was well received because everyone uses the RIR Protocol, so the speaker didn't take offense. She opened up an opportunity to make the situation right rather than condemning anyone.

By making the RIR Protocol part of everyone's professional common practice, the district has created a safe space for people to engage in tough conversations and build proficiency with repairing inequities. This approach has set the tone across the organization. There's no longer any excuse to avoid these conversations. Everyone has the tools and is expected to use them. The implementation has been a positive experience in shifting the climate, culture, how people interact, and how leaders lead.

It's human nature to want to repair *people* rather than issues. In special education, educators talk about separating the disability from the child. One way of doing so involves using "child-first language." For example, you say, "I have a student who is deaf," rather than "I have a deaf student." The disability doesn't have to define the child.

The same applies to people in general. When someone says or does something harmful, using that isolated behavior as an indicator of their value closes off opportunities for growth and repair. If we instead understand that they're simply exhibiting a behavior and behaviors can change, we preserve their humanity and our connection. If I write someone off as a bad person, there's no room for repair. If I compassionately convey that I don't like a behavior but that they're not an inherently bad person, then we can progress.

Separate the problem from the person. The person did

something, but that behavior is not all-defining. When we make it all-defining, suddenly an off-the-cuff comment made in ignorance or momentary anger can condemn someone for the rest of their life, which is, at its worst, what people mean by cancel culture.

By contrast, with the RIR Protocol, people have room to say, "Okay, I made a mistake. And I can do better." If people didn't allow me to grow, I'd still be a liar, as I described in the intrapersonal chapter. My own experiences of owning my mistakes and receiving forgiveness and grace to do better have reinforced to me that there is a better way than canceling people. Forgiveness has allowed me to see that my behavior doesn't have to define me and has created a pathway for me to be more forgiving and understanding. Having room to mess up and reflect helps us have empathy for ourselves and others. Part of our problem as a society is that people can't forgive others because they can't forgive themselves.

In the cases when someone doesn't forgive me, the RIR is still effective. The repair is for me to continue on the path of engaging, observing, and growing. I can interrupt through my own discomfort in not living up to my values and choose not to put myself in that position anymore, whether or not the other person gives me that grace. I can demonstrate to myself, and maybe even to them over time, that my mistake was an isolated moment and doesn't define who I am.

EQUITABLE ORGANIZATION CHARTS

When I started my business, everything happened backward. I began working without a business plan. As I added employees, there was no real strategy. I knew what my values and my mission were, but I hadn't articulated them. It was year four before I started setting long-term goals and asking what the strategic plan for Epoch would be. What do we want to accomplish? Who are we? What does it look like to put our mission and values into words?

In the process of answering those questions, we needed to create an organizational chart. When I finally did, it looked like every other org chart, and it felt wrong. I realized that the fact that it *was* like every other org chart I had ever seen was part of the problem. There I was at the top of a pyramid, with everyone at the bottom. If we're talking about equity, how do we eliminate the unequal power dynamic? I'm always going to be the boss, but how can we create an organizational flow that speaks to the value of every role in the organization? I knew I could not share it until I could speak to my concerns.

At a CEO retreat, I was sharing my concerns with another CEO in the training, and he shared that he liked to think of organizational structures as a soccer field. As a former athlete, that analogy resonated with me. It was a level field and every role mattered to the success of the team. So, I spent two days envisioning my entire team on the soccer field. I had my forwards, my midfielders, and my back fielders. (Now you soccer players, don't hold me accountable if my language is a little off!) I matched every role with a position in the organization. Then, I proposed it to my team. I called it an ecosystem rather than an organizational chart because an ecosystem is organic, changes, and grows, and it was important to recognize the impact of language in conveying information.

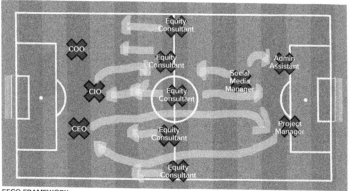

EECO FRAMEWORK

My forwards were my administrative assistant, webmaster, and program manager. They busted their butts to handle all the incoming contacts and make sure we looked good. My midfielders were the six consultants in the field doing the training. They were able to do their job because the forwards did theirs, setting up the meetings, arranging travel, and allowing the midfielders to focus on the midfield: being in the sessions, coaching, and training staff without worrying about all the logistics. In the backfield, you'd find me (the CEO), the COO, and (sometimes, LOL) my sister, who co-founded Epoch, doing the business development.

With those roles defined, I started drawing arrows and showing how we each moved. Sometimes my forwards have to understand what the midfielders are doing, which creates a fluid motion. I'm also a midfielder, because even though I'm the CEO, I'm also a trainer. I understand what the trainers need. As I'm negotiating contracts and talking about curriculum and programming, I'm clear on the impact for the midfield. One of my midfielders is a director. She's a trainer who also trains all the other trainers to make sure they're ready, and she builds client relationships. I explained that if you remove any player from the field, the game falls apart. We didn't actually have a traditional organization; we had a level playing field. No one is dispensable, because the minute we're down a player, someone else has to fill in and provide support. Every role truly counts.

I also wanted my team to understand that because we move fluidly and support each other, we all have some valuable perspective and experience on each role. Every voice counts. Just because you're a forward doesn't mean you can't talk to me at the backfield. You could very well have valuable feedback about an issue I don't fully see. Once I laid all this out, one of the consultants shared that she never thought she'd work in an organization where her voice both mattered and was so necessary. Having that structure within our organization is integral to our work, because otherwise we risk recreating, on some levels, a system of oppression. We are not perfect, but we've created an ecosystem that is forever evolving and changing. In this space, everyone knows that they have a voice and are expected to use it—even if it seems contradictory to what they think I want.

GENERATING BUY-IN

Using the RIR Protocol at an organizational level is challenging. Just because I recognize an issue doesn't mean other people do, too. For systems to change, you have to get buy-in. Building buy-in is where relationships come in. They're important on all three levels. To get you to buy in and help change something, I have to make a compelling argument for it. The most compelling arguments are personal. When people want to raise money for organizations with a social cause, from kids facing cancer to diabetes, they use personal narratives. Those stories motivate people to act. Very few people connect with the big picture. Instead, they connect on the individual level.

For example, I did the Komen three-day walk for breast cancer, which my sister-in-law had at the time. We eventually lost her to leukemia, which was a side effect of the chemo from the breast cancer, but at the time, she was still alive. In order to walk, you have to raise $2,500. If you don't raise it, you have to pay it yourself. The money comes from you one way or another, and that's how the organization fundraises. I wanted to raise it from others to build awareness, so I sent out a first request to my close friends. One of them responded and asked to share it with his circle, to which I said yes. He then told me not to limit my appeal to close friends because you never know who's been impacted by breast cancer and who would want to support this walk.

I took his comment to heart and decided to send a request to my entire contacts list, which was about 4,500 people at the time. I didn't expect people I hadn't connected with in a few years to respond; I was actually feeling a little sheepish about it but believed deeply in the cause, so I did it. The outpouring of support and loving comments astounded me. I raised close to $8,000 by myself. People I hadn't spoken to recently wrote back to say they'd lost someone they loved to cancer or someone they loved was a survivor. In that moment, I realized how many people have been touched by this disease and I knew I had made the right decision by offering the opportunity for those in pain to heal some of that pain through supporting an amazing cause.

I'd initially made a judgment about who would be responsive, but when I reached out, I found many more people than I expected felt a connection to the story of my sister-in-law. The issue also connected to their stories about loved ones. That shared bond led them to contribute. Hearing my story triggered something in them, which led to their action of making donations.

When we think about the issues closest to our heart, regardless of what side we're on, there's a trigger. We can always tie the situation back to a pain point in our life. If we can tap into that pain point, then we can help people expand and grow from that space. On the other hand, if we don't acknowledge the human experience and instead fixate on big, lofty ideas, we get less movement.

My organizational work all stems from a personal motivation. Even though I'm working at a systemic level, I emphasize relationships. The students I impact are people's children. They're like my nieces and nephews. These are our babies. Everything I do comes from that understanding. When we think about using the RIR Protocol, we see what seems to be technical policies and procedures, but those have a real impact on people's lives.

When we can connect the necessary systemic changes to a personal experience or an individual, we begin to get buy-in and see movement. If the RIR Protocol allows me to recognize my feelings about hiring practices, and I see that everyone in leadership is mostly White and male, then I can translate my frustration and anger into a productive interruption. I can ask how the system could become more inclusive, so I don't feel those negative emotions. I can consider how we might become more inclusive of other perspectives that will support different policies and procedures. Diversifying the leaders who make the decisions leads to concrete impacts on individual children, families, and communities. Everything is connected.

We don't change policies and procedures simply for the sake of changing them. Using the RIR Protocol as a framework, we change them because they're not achieving what they should be. If we can get in touch with what they should be doing and how they're missing the mark, then we can reach consensus about a repair.

One of my colleagues said that a very conservative, right-wing friend of hers posted a list of what she wanted in life, which she saw as justifying her support of Donald Trump. I looked at the list and realized of the fifteen items, I wanted thirteen of them. I want my children to be safe. I want respect, dignity, and freedom. We're not as different as we think we are. Underneath the political designations, we have the same basic desires and needs for our families and communities. Can we start from the common ground and then come up with solutions together that would be mutually beneficial, instead of thinking if one person gains, another person has to lose?

Through using the RIR Protocol, we can find connection with people who seem extremely different from us at first.

We can find connection and buy-in to bridge those divides. The steps aren't necessarily intuitive, but through practice, we can reach that understanding. We're *all* capable of getting there. The RIR Protocol is a way to support taking what isn't intuitive and making it so.

SPEAKING UP

Ultimately, Nicole's textbook rubric rollout led to an amazing meeting. She said the team had their best discussion on record. They were honest about the shortcomings in different texts, and they spoke candidly about what they were looking for and how to approach finding that kind of book. She calibrated the rubric with them. Then, when companies sent them sample textbooks, they could rank the options and decide which to purchase.

One company felt fairly confident it would get the contract. Based on the rubric, though, the team found that the textbook was still horrible, even though on the surface, it appeared better and more inclusive. It still centered Whiteness and told a very colonial version of history. The people of color stayed relegated to the sidebars or margins. So, the district turned it down. The company reps asked what was wrong with their offering, and she ended up sharing the rubric with them at their request.

The rubric allowed her team to recognize the problem with

the textbook, interrupt by not settling for adopting it, and tell the company why. The repair was significant in that the company invited her team to be part of an advisory board to rewrite the textbooks, because Nicole's school district is huge. It spends millions of dollars on books, so retaining it as a customer and meeting its needs was important to the publisher.

The experience demonstrated the potential for leveraging power for good. Nicole's team reached an agreement with the company to accept a textbook if it underwent particular revisions to align with the rubric. The process was quite complicated and expensive because any changes also needed state approval. When the textbook rolled out, Nicole saw that some of the agreed-upon changes *still* hadn't occurred, so she called and asked for corrections, which cost the company another $250,000 just for her district. She says the books still aren't perfect but using the RIR Protocol led to dramatic improvements and a major victory for equitable curriculum.

Her one district impacted anyone using those textbooks in the entire state of California. That solution carries tremendous power, and it originated with the RIR Protocol steps of recognize, interrupt, and repair. Nicole stayed the course, knowing the two sides could come to a valuable agreement if they were willing to dig in and work together. That commitment, in turn, had a ripple effect for so many people beyond her immediate organization.

PAUSE AND PRACTICE

- What are some of the issues you notice within your organization that are problematic?

- Who is impacted by said issues?

- Who benefits by keeping the practice in place?

- Do you feel empowered to address them with the necessary parties?

- If not, what gets in the way of you doing so?

CHAPTER 7

WHY SHOULD WE MOVE FORWARD WITH URGENCY?

In 2017, an activist named Bree Newsome climbed a thirty-foot flagpole outside the South Carolina statehouse and took down the confederate flag that flew there. There she was, a Black woman, high in the air, shouting, "You come against me with hatred, oppression, and violence," a news outlets reported.[8] "I come against you in the name of God. This flag comes down today."

On the ground, though, a far less quotable conversation was

---

8   Lottie Joiner, "Bree Newsome Reflects on Taking Down South Carolina's Confederate Flag 2 Years Ago," *Vox*, June 27, 2017, https://www.vox.com/identities/2017/6/27/15880052/bree-newsome-south-carolinas-confederate-flag.

happening. Officers were discussing how to stop Newsome; how to get her down. Bystanders reported that they heard the officers decide to tase the metal pole Newsome clung to, high above. Such an act surely would have caused her to lose her grip and fall, likely to her death.

But they didn't tase it. Why? Because a White man standing next to the pole—a White man who had accompanied Bree to the statehouse that day and who supported her mission—reached out and grabbed the pole once he heard the plan. Nobody talks about that man, but I think often about how he saved Bree's life. They were in it together. Both of them knew, at some level, that there had to be a White man there while a Black woman made that climb. There had to be someone there willing to utilize his privilege in order for a revolutionary act to happen; for a marginalized voice to be heard.

When are we, as people, willing to put our hands on the proverbial pole?

Allyship in itself is extremely valuable, but there is a time when allyship must shift to co-conspiratorship. That's what James Ian Tyson did with Bree. It is that time now, for us, as a society. It has been that time for a long while, to tell you the truth, but there's no denying that we've reached a social and political inflection point at the time of this writing. If things were going to change on their own, they would have already. Not only can we not afford to go backward, but we also cannot afford to languish in this new status quo rooted in discomfort and division. That division takes a toll on us as humans—we are more unhappy, lonelier, and less secure than the generation before us. We can no longer sit on the sidelines of change, and each of us has to find our way to be accomplices for those who are most marginalized. The only way is forward, with urgency and fervor. Together.

And look, you may not have it in you to do what James Ian Tyson did. That's okay. But there *are* actions you can take that can significantly impact an outcome with some thought and intention. As Dr. Asa Hilliard said, we need "will, skill and desire," with desire being a critical component.

We need to be vocal—and not just people of color. It's time we see hands of all colors on that pole. How we make that happen starts by putting what you've learned so far into practice.

In a moment, we'll take a closer look at what that looks like.

WHAT'S NEXT?

More practice. As we've moved through this book together, I've left a series of "Pause and Practice" questions for you to reflect upon. Let's review them once more and if you haven't already, answer them for yourself:

PAUSE AND PRACTICE

CHAPTER 1

- What is an issue that is unresolved that you have been carrying around with you?

- What do you think is the impact on your body and mind if you continue to carry it?

- What gets in the way of you resolving the issue?

- What would it mean to you to not have to think about it anymore?

CHAPTER 2

- Re-read the four communication styles. What type of communicator are you?

- Which of the Four Affects do you typically default to?

- How do the two combined impact the way you communicate?

- How do the two combined impact the way you hear others?

- What communication style triggers you the most? How does that show up in your life?

- What are some steps you can take to reduce those triggers and strengthen your communication with the particular style and/or affect?

CHAPTER 3

- What feelings did these sample statements trigger in you?

- What would be your typical reaction if you had not used the RIR Protocol?

- If your reaction involved defensiveness or aggression, would it have had the impact you wanted?

- Could there be another way?

- Now that you've identified your feelings, I'm going to invite you to pick one statement and think about how you could interrupt. Here are the four statements again:
  - "There is no White privilege. I grew up poor, and my family worked hard for everything we had."
  - "Why are you acting like a girl?"
  - "That's gay."
  - "You are so articulate."

- Here are the stems again:
  - "Tell me more about that."
  - "I want to understand."
  - "What does that mean to you?"
  - "What has been your experience with _____?"
  - "I've had a different experience with _____."
  - "I have a different perspective on _____."
  - "I think your intention was positive, but what you said felt _____ to me. Can we talk about it more?"
  - "I hear your frustration. How do you think we can address that?"

- What did you "Recognize" about your feelings?

- How would/could you "Interrupt"?

CHAPTER 4

- Of all the identities you have, which ones bring you joy?

- Which ones have you had to alter the most?

- Which one has been the most consistent over your lifetime?

- Which one creates the greatest risk to you?

- Which one brings you the greatest safety?

- Are there relationships you can think of that you have some unresolved issue with?

- How much time do you spend thinking about the person or the issue?

- What gets in the way of you addressing the issue with the person?

CHAPTER 6

- What are some of the issues you notice within your organization that are problematic?

- Who is impacted by said issues?

- Who benefits by keeping the practice in place?

- Do you feel empowered to address them with the necessary parties?

- If not, what gets in the way of you doing so?

TAKE THE FIRST STEP

The call being asked of us all now is to move beyond talk and toward action. So, I ask you, what are you willing to do? To sacrifice? Whatever change you are seeking, now is the time to pursue it.

We can start that journey by answering some basic questions: What moves us? To what issues do we feel most connected? What type of potential change lights us up inside? What issue or problem weighs on our heart and deserves more of our energy?

Once you identify what it is that you feel called to address, you have an opportunity to act. But first, I get it—I understand that you may not feel ready to take this big step. However, I want to plant a seed in you that you can nurture after you develop a little more skill using the RIR Protocol, which you will shortly. For now, remember...you are not alone nor without direction; you have the RIR Protocol to help you.

Use the guiding questions below to unpack an issue you want to attend to. You will get more practice with scenarios shortly, but I want you to see and understand the type of impact you *can* have once you build the RIR Protocol into your daily practice.

Recognize

Recognize It

- What have you recognized either personally or professionally that you have a desire to impact or change?
- What have you already tried?
- What else can be done?

Interrupt

Interrupt It

- Who can you collaborate with as a thought partner and/or co-conspirator?
- What questions do you need to ask and of whom?
- What learning do you have to do to prepare yourself?

Repair

Repair It

- How do you stay engaged in the change process?
- How do you bring others along with you?
- How do you keep compassion front and center?

Now that we're reminded of the context, let's practice by drawing a card. We'll do one together, and then I invite you to continue on your own using the same steps.

PRACTICING TOGETHER: THE CONVERSATION STARTER CARDS™ IN ACTION

Below you will find four sample cards for your practice.

STEP ONE: FACE A TRIGGER

I would like you to read each and then choose the one that triggers you the most. This is important because if the statement doesn't trigger you, there is no reason to act. In addition, choosing the easy one will not give you the depth of practice needed to really lean in when the conversation turns south.

They're just looking for a handout.

If we hire any more of them, they're going to take over.

My family was poor and we didn't act like that.

If she doesn't want to be harassed, she should dress differently.

STEP TWO: RECOGNIZE IT

Choose the card you are going to focus on. Ask yourself the following questions and write down your answers:

- What is the initial feeling that comes up for you when you hear the statement? (Refer to the Feeling Wheel if you have trouble.)
- Where do you feel it in your body?

- Without riding your emotional wave, what would your normal reaction be?
- Would that reaction yield your desired outcome?
- What feeling did you recognize?

STEP THREE: INTERRUPT IT

Choose one of sample stems listed here[9] to interrupt the statement or create your own in your own voice to interrupt. Write down what you chose.

- "What does that mean to you?"
- "I've had a different experience with _____."
- "Tell me more about that."

What statement did you use to interrupt?

STEP FOUR: REPAIR IT

Remember, repair can only happen AFTER you have interrupted and depends entirely on how the interruption went. If the interruption went well, the repair can be as simple as reengaging later by saying hello and asking a question to start a new dialogue. If the interruption was difficult, it might require some deeper work.

---

9   A full list of strategies and stems for interrupting is available in Chapter 3 as well as in the Appendix.

Think about the card you chose and the interruption you used. Which strategy for repair[10] might be the best for you to reengage with the person from the card? Should new boundaries be created? Can collective learning happen? Will this repair mean divorce?

What type of repair did you decide on?

WHAT'S NEXT?

Compassionate Dialogue™ is work, but it's important work. The practice in this chapter proves that. It's important to keep strengthening your RIR muscle.

Now, remember that issue I had you think about earlier? It's time to act. I encourage you to move to the RIR Protocol worksheet in the Appendix, which walks you through the process, and use it to work through your personal issue. Let's go!

---

10   A full list of strategies and stems for repairing is available in Chapter 3 as well as in the Appendix.

CONCLUSION

By the time you close this book, I hope you feel empowered to act, starting with yourself and your intrapersonal journey. I hope you're already asking yourself what kind of communicator you are and whether you've been leaning too hard on passivity or aggression. I hope the wheels are already turning: is your communication as effective as you want it to be? How could you make it more effective?

Engaging with compassion requires critical self-reflection and self-understanding. The tools I've laid out can help you deepen your relationship with yourself and your truth through practice.

Practice, of course, is an *action*—an action that requires the desire to change. And even though this action and reflection are not easy, they are important. If you've gotten this far, I know you believe that, too.

Don't overthink this. At this stage, my goal for you is that you can walk away feeling reflective and capable of changing how you engage. You now have another tool in your toolkit. That's it! You don't need any special strategy. You just need the desire and then the willingness to try and practice. I designed the RIR Protocol to be approachable for this very reason.

You can do this. Don't fall back into the political correctness trap.

People who focus on political correctness tend to have compassionate hearts, but they don't get the results they're looking for. Stifling conversations won't help us grow. We have to break down those barriers to connection, starting within ourselves and then working our way up to the larger systems at play. Change starts within us, and then we can bring that new perspective to our interactions with others. No matter how large our goals for the world, the intrapersonal work is a lifelong piece of the puzzle. Remember, Compassionate Dialogue™ is not only about how to initiate engagement with others but also how we receive feedback and criticism. Our growth and development are incumbent on our ability to be vulnerable and lean into discomfort. We will not always like what we hear but if we can put our egos aside and listen differently, we may be able to understand a differing perspective and, in some cases, find that we have been given an opportunity to grow.

So, what's the first small step you can take today?

If applicable, who will you use your privilege to protect?

How will you use the RIR Protocol in the short term? The long term?

What change will you be a part of making?

We started this book by asking a seemingly simple question: "Why can't we just talk?" Perhaps the answer to that question is and always has been there: we *can* talk if that talking is through Compassionate Dialogue™.

Continue to the Appendix to find more resources and information as you navigate difficult conversations.

APPENDICES

4 Types of Communicators:

Functional	Analytical
INTUITIVE	Personal

4 Types of Affects

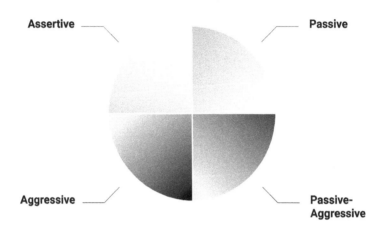

Assertive

Passive

Aggressive

Passive-
Aggressive

APPENDIX 3

Functional	Analytical
INTUITIVE	**Personal**

APPENDIX 4

EPOCH
EDUCATION

Functional	**Analytical**
INTUITIVE	**Personal**

1 Identify your primary communication style based on the 4 types and write #1 in the box.

2 Identify your secondary communication style based on the 4 types and write #2 in the box.

3 Identify your primary affect and write it in the pie piece that corresponds with your primary style.

4 Identify your secondary affect and write in the pie piece that corresponds with your secondary style.

5 List your communication characteristics that apply to your identified styles.

6 Identify the styles and characteristics that trigger you most.

APPENDIX 6

Characteristic	Acceptable	Approaching	Concerning	Very Problematic
The authors of the materials represent diverse backgrounds and perspectives.	All of the following groups are represented in the authorship panels: • Women • People of color • LGBTQ people • People with disabilities Representation extends beyond "tokenism."	Most of the following groups are represented in the authorship panels: • Women • People of color • LGBTQ people • People with disabilities	A token person or two who belong(s) to the following groups is/are represented on the authorship panels: • Women • People of color • LGBTQ people • People with disabilities	The entire panel is exclusively white and male.
People of color and other diverse communities are central to the narrative, rather than (literally) marginalized in the periphery of the pages.	The main copy tells rich stories throughout every unit, chapter, and section about the historical contributions of diverse communities. Peripheral materials add to the richness of the text.	There are stories about the historical contributions of diverse communities in every chapter and unit. Peripheral materials include more examples than the main text.	There are one or two examples of diverse communities in each chapter. The stories take up very little physical space in the main copy.	There are very few examples of historical contributions of diverse communities in the text. Examples of diverse communities are primarily left to the notes, margins, sidebar coverage, captions, and/or supplemental materials.
People of color and other diverse communities "tell" their own stories in these materials.	Wherever possible, the stories about diverse people are told in their own words (e.g., through primary sources or other tools and narratives that are authored by people with diverse identities).	There are some primary sources from the perspective of diverse individuals and communities included throughout the materials.	There are only a few examples of primary sources written by diverse individuals or communities. A significant portion of the primary source documents included in the materials are still authored by white men.	The stories about diverse individuals are primarily told through the textbook author's words (in the main copy of the text or in the sidebar material). These authors are primarily white men.

Characteristic	Acceptable	Approaching	Concerning	Very Problematic
The materials offer perspectives from all or most groups impacted by historical events and periods.	Multiple perspectives of an issue are thoroughly discussed and explored. Multiple perspectives are complex enough to help students develop a well-rounded understanding of historical events, issues, and time periods.	Multiple perspectives of an issue are included; perhaps one perspective is emphasized a little more than others. Perspectives shared are varied.	There may be one or two alternative perspectives included in the materials. The materials still favor the dominant culture's traditional view of the historical events. Perspectives shared are superficial and perhaps slightly misleading.	The materials reinforce the superiority of the dominant culture's viewpoint.
People of color and members of other diverse communities are seen as people with power who have shaped history rather than primarily as victims.	Most of the examples of diverse individuals are portrayed as decision makers and leaders, not as passive recipients of the dominant culture's decisions. The materials include more than the "typical" examples of diverse heroes; students learn about diverse people that are usually absent from history curriculum. The historical significance of diverse people and communities are explained and discussed in robust ways.	There are some examples of people of color being portrayed as decision-makers and leaders, but the materials still incorporate more examples of diverse individuals fighting oppression. While students may still see "typical" examples of diverse heroes; students may be introduced to some new historical figures. Contributions of diverse people and communities are explained.	There are a few examples of diverse leaders in powerful situations, but most of the examples of these leaders are related to victimization. The materials list names of diverse individuals who have impacted history; they are the typical figures that tend to be included in history books. Contributions of diverse people and communities are listed, but not explained.	The materials include simply a token list of names of diverse individuals who have impacted history. Examples of diverse people in leadership roles primarily portray people who have been victimized and are fighting oppression. Contributions of diverse people are difficult to find or misrepresented.

APPENDIX 7

Corporate Equity Walk-Through Tool

How Inclusive is Your Brand?

Brand Identity/Messaging

Consider the following when assessing diversity and inclusion at the Brand Identity/Messaging level:

- Does your brand's mission, vision, or values use language that emphasizes the importance of diversity, equity, and inclusion?

- Who are your current clients/customers? How could you expand your definition of "target audience" to make it more inclusive and diverse?

- Is your brand/marketing team representative of the population you serve? Are they a diverse group of people?

- Do you actively research and interview minority groups when developing brand strategies or marketing campaigns?

- Does your messaging address the topics of inclusion and equity or discuss topics related to diversity and identity?

- Does your brand seek opportunities to address the needs of unique or marginalized populations or break down stereotypes? (e.g., Microsoft developing customized game controllers for those with physical disabilities or missing limbs making it difficult to play video games with traditional equipment; the Always #Like a Girl campaign, or Nike's Pro Hijab campaign for Muslim women)

Marketing Assets/Channels

Review all customer/client-facing marketing materials or channels (website, print media, social media, presentations, etc.) that you utilize using this checklist. Note where you are doing well, could use improvement, or are missing the mark.

Sample "Interruptions" might include:

- Are always inclusive and diverse; whenever possible and appropriate, visuals include a broad representation of ethnicities, gender identities/roles, sexual orientations, physical abilities, family structures, socioeconomic statuses, community representations, etc.

- Consider role assignment and portrayal to ensure visual is not promoting racist, sexist, ageist, homophobic, or other stereotypes. (e.g., women always doing the cleaning, romance always heterosexual)

- Actively uses "nontraditional" role assignment and portrayal to break down stereotypes (a gay couple with their children, a model with physical disability, etc.)

- Do not use visual representations or iconography associated with a specific culture for purposes that are unintended by the original culture or offensive to that culture's mores.

Marketing Assets/Channels cont.

Written content:

- Does not contain language that may be construed as offensive or off-putting to segments of the population

- Does not artificially co-opt words or phrases unique to ethnic or cultural populations (i.e., verbal/written cultural appropriation)

- Avoids use of colloquialisms whenever possible to promote inclusivity

- Uses slang or trending terms with great care and only when appropriate

- Uses gender-neutral pronouns when/where appropriate

- Uses the primary language of the target audience, but always adjusts to in-market language whenever possible

Digital content (website, social media, blog, community platforms):

- Follows all guidelines above for both written and visual content

- Is 501-compliant where applicable (i.e., persons with disabilities can use your website without difficulty)

- Uses inclusive design principles (text is readable; images have alt-text and captions; videos are captioned and have transcripts; color contrast is set to 4:5:1; color is not relied upon for meaning (color-blind), etc.)

APPENDIX 8

Physical Environment: Acknowledging and Connectedness

Title	Possible Examples	Notes	Rating
1. Displays represent diverse cultural materials, photos, words, art. There are positive representations of the racial and cultural identities of students represented within the school.	• Wall displays are more than cartoon representations of diversity • Students "see" themselves in the room • Displays recognize contributions of a diverse population • Real life imagery is used to convey messaging		
2. High quality student work is displayed.	• Students have a say in their work that is represented on the wall • Diverse examples of excellence are represented on the walls • Work is fresh, new, rotated		

N/A: did not observe   1. absent   2. saw occasionally   3. saw consistently   4. saw outstanding examples of

Physical Environment: Acknowledging and Connectedness

Title	Possible Examples	Notes	Rating
3. Classroom climate is warm and welcoming to students.	• Teacher greets each student by name • Engaging learning opportunities are visible • Classroom "feels" like a place different learners want to learn in		
4. Classroom environment is conducive to collaborative learning.	• Flexible grouping opportunities are visible • Flexible seating opportunities are visible • Easy flow and space to move about		
5. Literature (class libraries) reflects the cultural diversity of the students in the class and of the greater society.	• Books are independently accessible to students • Random sampling of books reflect multiple identities • There are more than "just a few" diverse books • Diverse literature goes beyond biographies and non-fiction representation		

N/A: did not observe   1. absent   2. saw occasionally   3. saw consistently   4. saw outstanding examples of

Physical Environment: Acknowledging and Connectedness

Title	Possible Examples	Notes	Rating
6. Students feel like they belong in the classroom and the classroom belongs to them.	• Students are known and celebrated as individuals with rich cultural and racial identities • Students have confidence with procedures and routines • Students take leadership roles in the class • Classroom rules reflect student input		
7. Students problem solve independently.	• Students know where to look to get answers to their questions • Teacher recognizes what students need to develop their own executive function		

N/A: did not observe   1. absent   2. saw occasionally   3. saw consistently   4. saw outstanding examples of

Physical Environment: Acknowledging and Connectedness

Title	Possible Examples	Notes	Rating
8. Resources are available and easily accessed.	• Classroom supports students' independence through accessible resources • Resources that students need to use daily are available and accessible to them		
9. Opportunities for independence and autonomy are available.	• Students know what to do when they are done with assignments • Classroom activities are set up so students can manage their time and behavior		

N/A: did not observe   1. absent   2. saw occasionally   3. saw consistently   4. saw outstanding examples of

APPENDIX 9

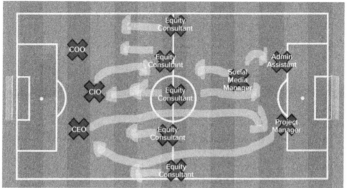

EECO FRAMEWORK

RIR Protocol

Recognize It

The objective is to recognize what we think, feel, and believe about statements and actions that perpetuate separation, exclusion, and deficit thinking. Answering these questions helps us pause in order to thoughtfully respond instead of reacting. Ask yourself:

1. What is my physical response? (ex. stomach clenching, throat tightening)
2. How do I feel? What emotion does this evoke?
3. What is my initial belief or story about this?

Interrupt It

The objective is to engage in a way that creates open, honest dialogue around difficult issues. For example, what can I ask to understand the person's intent? How can I be empathetic as well as share how this impacts me?

1. Ask to clarify meaning
2. Ask to understand intent
3. Address the deed instead of condemning the doer
4. Address the impact
5. Offer another perspective/share why it's important to you
6. Acknowledge the speaker and connect with empathy
7. Seek to include in ongoing dialogue

Sample "Interruptions" might include:

- "Tell me more about that, I want to understand."
- "What does that mean to you?"
- "What has been your experiece with _____?"
- "I've had a different experience with _____."
- "I have a different perspective on _____."
- "I think your intention was positive, but what you said felt _____ to me. Can we talk about it more?"
- "I hear your frustration. That was challenging for me as well…"
- "How do you think we can address that?"

Repair It

The objective is to come up with actionable steps that invite connection and inclusion, keep the issue on the table until it is resolved, and create sustainable change.

Observe: Seek solutions that expand your understanding of the issue—attend community events or groups, films, music, etc.

Engage: Continuously interact with different people and perspectives—seek or be an ally, model respectful engagement, follow-up on difficult interactions, take responsibility for your actions.

Study: Deepen your knowledge and ability to discuss the issue—research the issue, take a course or book study, offer to learn together, bring the issue to a larger group or staff meeting.

RECOGNIZE IT

Personal: _____

Professional: _____

INTERRUPT IT

Personal: _____

Professional: _____

REPAIR IT

Personal: _____

Professional: _____

APPENDIX 11

Epoch Enterprise 20 Day Compassionate Dialogue Challenge
epochenterprise20dayequitychallenge.prohabits.com
https://qrco.de/bcbFzB

Start page url:
https://20daycompassionatedialogue.prohabits.com/start

We would like to invite you on a journey to become an active force in creating equitable spaces personally and professionally.

No sign-ups, no passwords. Only takes a few minutes per day.

Epoch 20-Day Equity Challenges provide daily opportunities to practice, explore and expand your ability to engage with a variety of equity topics.

We know that making equity sustainable is like building muscle. Committing to our daily microactivities builds your knowledge and confidence to be an active participant in creating positive change in your environments.

Epoch Education (For Educators)
Epocheducation20dayequitychallenge.prohabits.com
https://qrco.de/equitychallenge

Start page url:
https://epocheducation20dayequitychallenge.prohabits.com/start

They're just looking for a handout.

If we hire any more of them, they're going to take over.

My family was poor and we didn't act like that.

If she doesn't want to be harassed, she should dress differently.

Note: For more information about bringing Compassionate Dialogue™ to a school or organization, and to purchase Conversation Starter Cards™, please visit www.epoch education.com.

ABOUT THE AUTHOR

DR. NANCY DOME is an educator at heart, not just in practice. Everything she does is for the betterment of those around her...her community and ultimately the world. Dr. Dome has always had a desire to be of service to others and believes it is her responsibility to be the change she wants to see.

As a part of bringing that vision to life, Nancy has been a mentor to ten amazing kids over the past seven years and is grateful to help increase their opportunities for success through honesty, love, and guidance. This endeavor has not occurred in a vacuum, as young people are Dr. Dome's North Star. She has continued to serve in various capacities to positively impact as many of their lives as possible, always keeping civil rights as it relates to access issues for marginalized youth at the forefront of her efforts. A snapshot of those efforts includes the following:

- As a board member and president for Dollars for Scholars, which provides students in alternative education programs access to college scholarships; and
- As a board member for Teen Services Sonoma, which provides training to teens around workplace readiness; and
- As a board member for Hanna Boys Center, which is a residential program for at risk boys that provides services to youth, families, and communities impacted by trauma and adversity through resilience, connection, and spiritual wellness; and
- As a current board member for Positive Coaching Alliance, which is dedicated to cultivating a positive youth sports culture.

Outside—or, more likely, as a core driver—of this work with youth, Dr. Dome is a natural people person and has always gravitated toward personal interactions and experiences that help her grow to be a better human and expose her to different cultures. Traveling, for instance, has been a passion of Nancy's since she was seventeen years old and discovered that a plane ticket and some ingenuity could get you almost anywhere. She has been lucky enough to travel most of the world and to live abroad in England, Belgium, and the Dominican Republic, where she met some of the most amazing people on the planet.

In her past life, Nancy was a professional volleyball player, and she credits her higher education pursuits and successes to that talent. Being able to do something she loved that allowed her to get all her degrees either through playing or coaching has been a gift and a blessing. Furthermore, those experiences taught her the value of hard work and teamwork—lessons that still serve her today. Ultimately, sports taught her that we are better together.

Personally, Nancy loves being in nature, enjoying intimate gatherings where compassionate humans get to lean in with one another, and photographing special moments. She is the proud godmother of five (Nick, Grant, Sophia, Julius, and Olivia), the proud dog momma of Abby, and the happy wife to Taylor.

If you would like to keep up to date on what Nancy is doing and the projects she has in the wings—which could even be her next book—reach out at drnancydome.com.